TEACHING CRITICAL

TELEVISION VIEWING

SKILLS

TEACHING CRITICAL TELEVISION VIEWING SKILLS

An Integrated Approach

By

MILTON E. PLOGHOFT

Ohio University
Athens, Ohio

and

JAMES A. ANDERSON

University of Utah
Salt Lake City, Utah

CHARLES   C   THOMAS   •   PUBLISHER
Springfield • Illinois • U.S.A.

Published and Distributed Throughout the World by

CHARLES C THOMAS • PUBLISHER

2600 South First Street

Springfield, Illinois, 62717, U.S.A.

© *1982 by* CHARLES C THOMAS • PUBLISHER

ISBN 0-398-04616-6

Library of Congress Catalog Card Number: 81-16704

.

With THOMAS BOOKS *careful attention is given to all details of manufacturing and
design. It is the Publisher's desire to present books that are satisfactory as to their physical
qualities and artistic possibilities and appropriate for their particular use.* THOMAS
BOOKS *will be true to those laws of quality that assure a good name and good will.*

Printed in the United States of America
CU-RX-1

Library of Congress Cataloging in Publication Data

Ploghoft, Milton E.
   Teaching critical television viewing skills.

   Bibliography: p.
   Includes index.
   1. Television and children. 2. Television in educa-
tion. 3. Television programs--Evaluation. I. Anderson,
James A. II. Title.
HQ784.T4P53   371.3'358   81-16704
ISBN 0-398-04616-6   AACR2

FOREWORD

SINCE 1949, when television began its rapid penetration of American society, there has been a continuing concern for the effects television viewing could have on young people. After many attempts by various groups to influence the kinds of programs shown on television, and with the explosion of programs by way of Home Box Office, super satellite stations, video discs, and other technological developments, the concern has not diminished.

This book began as a response to concerns over children and their uses of television. It was, and is, predicated on the conviction that it is better to educate people to live intelligently with the products of science and technology; to be informed masters, rather than naive slaves of television and its programs.

As we worked with many schools in the creation and testing of critical viewing skills curricula, it became obvious that the traditional skills of language arts and social studies formed the foundations for the specific skills appropriate to the analysis and evaluation of television program content.

This book provides direction to the integration of critical viewing skills into the regular curriculum. Learning experiences may be developed, using the activities provided here, for the attainment of basic viewing skills. Results from a recently concluded viewing skills project in Idaho Falls, Idaho, indicate that critical viewing skills instruction does make a difference in the behavior of children, and that basic language skills are enhanced in the process.

It is intended that this book will be a valuable resource in teacher education courses, as a basic guide for in-service courses, and as a classroom reference for teachers who are preparing young people to deal effectively with all of the mass media, print and electronic.

Milton E. Ploghoft
James A. Anderson

ACKNOWLEDGMENTS

MANY persons have contributed to the process that led to the writing of this book. Unfortunately, there is not sufficient space to properly recognize all of them for the various kinds of assistance they provided over many years. Certainly, we must acknowledge the parts played by the students, teachers, administrators, and parents of the schools in Eugene, Oregon; East Syracuse, New York; Idaho Falls, Idaho; Clark County, Nevada; and Belpre, Ohio. It was these districts where we were provided with the opportunities to develop and test our curriculum materials in critical television viewing as early as 1969.

School superintendents in those districts had the vision and courage to support this curriculum innovation at a time when it was more popular to limit efforts to the traditional basics; hence recognition must go to Dr. Millard Pond, Dr. Tom Payzant, Dr. James Parsley, Dr. Fritz Hess, and Dr. Claude Perkins.

The timely support of the George Gund Foundation made it possible to hold the first national conference on Children and Television: Implications for Education in 1979, and the information exchanged there provided important breadth and depth to the content of this book.

Finally, as with all such projects, the preparation of the manuscript required the patient and expert assistance of many key persons at Ohio University and the University of Utah. Especially must we express thanks to Joy Hemsley and Nancy Karnes, who saw to it that the last revisions and editorial changes were properly included.

M.E.P.
J.A.A.

CONTENTS

TEACHING CRITICAL TELEVISION VIEWING SKILLS

Chapter 1

CHILDREN, TELEVISION, AND RECEIVERSHIP SKILLS

INTRODUCTION

In the period 1952 to 1972, television went from "new toy" status to a permanent fixture in more than 90 percent of the households in the United States. Television is the single most attended medium. Throughout the world, television has been accepted as an exceedingly successful technological solution to the problem of distribution of news, information, and above all, entertainment.

Perhaps one reason for the success of television is that it is a preeminent means of communication because it closely duplicates the natural conditions of communication among people. Interpersonal contact is the foundation of human communication. It is through this contact that children acquire information concerning the behavior of people and begin to assign meaning and worth to a vast array of episodes and relationships. Long before children encounter the process of reading as an avenue to an infinite array of vicarious experiences, they have begun to develop their own personal concepts of right and wrong, love and hate, friend and stranger, good and bad from their social contacts with human behavior around them. Meanings are learned for facial expressions, gestures, tones of voice, manners of speaking, as well as for what is said. The language of children is this natural language, a human phenomenon that provides the basic vehicle by which human beings of one group or another can share the stories and meanings of their experiences.

Television uses all of the elements of natural language to sell, to inform, to entertain, and to persuade. Without the display of a single printed word, television informs the viewer as to the feelings, values, and motivations of a host of characters who appear in the situation comedies, in the commercials, and in the documentaries and news programs. Just as print literacy was never a requisite to learning the basic truths of the family or tribe in the preprint era, today's television programs make no demand on the skills of print literacy for the viewer to share in this communication process.

The fact that only the most commonplace skills are necessary to participate and enjoy the content of television presents us with a two-pronged problem: Children may be interacting with content without sufficient guidance, and the very easy access to television makes it difficult for all of us, adult and child alike, to use this medium in an intelligent and reflective manner. It is this problem that gives direction to efforts to develop viewing skills in our children.

RECEIVERSHIP SKILLS DEFINED

From work that was done in the early 1970s in Eugene, Oregon, and East Syracuse, New York, a core of viewing skills was identified as highly relevant to the acts of receivership, or critical viewing. These major skill areas are as follows:

  I. Comprehending the message
    Grasping the meaning of the message
    Comprehending language discriminately
    Comprehending images discriminately
    Interpreting "hidden" meanings
    Specifying the working element of the message
    Understanding to whom the message is directed
    Interpreting the intent of the message
  II. Perceiving the elements of the message
    Noting details of the message
    Noting sequence of the elements
    Perceiving relationship of elements
    Identifying character traits
    Noting integration of aural and visual elements
  III. Evaluating the message
    Assignment of credibility to statements
    Identifying fact, opinion, imaginative writing, and images
    Identifying affective appeals
    Evaluating logic, reasoning, and "montaged" relationships
  IV. Reacting to the message personally

Recognizing intended affective reactions and motives
Relegating personal value (utility) to the message
Drawing conclusions, inferences, or predictions
V. Comprehending the impact of medium
Understanding the role of television in one's life and impact
of this role on message
Understanding impact of the institutional structure of television on the message

Receivership skills begin with those skills needed to identify and understand our own motives and purposes for attending to TV programs. They include our ability to interpret the influence of our personal motives and purposes on the way we make sense of the messages we receive — that we may at the outset be more receptive to some content and less open to other ideas and images.

Receiver skills involve understandings that go beyond the surface meanings and permit us to analyze language and the visual and aural images in order to specify the working elements of each. This makes it possible to deal with the hidden meanings and intents of the message.

Receiver skills foster the observation of details, their sequence and relationships, in a purposeful manner to arrive at an understanding of the themes, values, motivating elements, plotlines, characters, and characterizations that appear in programs and commercials. They provide for a reflective evaluation of fact and opinion, logical and affective appeals, imaginative and creative writing, and images.

Receivership skills include an understanding of the distortions present in all media messages, which are inherent in the medium and in the grammar, syntax, and meanings and which are contained in the methods selected to produce this message.

Last, individuals trained in critical viewing skills will be equipped with criteria for evaluating intention, motives, and audience response, for assigning value or worth to the message for some purpose. These individuals can integrate the message and test it against other information bases. They can make inferences and draw conclusions.

At the outset it may be observed that these major skill

areas are clearly part of the traditional school program. "Comprehending the message" in the traditional frame of reference means "understanding what you have read." In the age of television, this must be extended to mean "understanding what you have heard and seen." "Perceiving the elements of a message" is a skill area that has been limited to the reading process, and, occasionally, to reportorial writing. Television viewing skill requires sharper attention to the elements of a televised message due to the fact that visual effects and other nonverbal elements must be attended to in addition to the aural elements.

"Evaluating the television message" requires skills similar to those needed to assign credibility, to identify affective appeals, and to separate fact from opinion in reading printed messages. Again, the medium of television presents a more complex array of "communicators" of meaning than does the printed medium, hence the need for skills that will enable the viewer to cope with more than the meanings of printed words.

Let us consider several of the objectives of the conventional language arts program and relate them to activities that make use of critical viewing skills.

- Listening skills, which include attending to intonation, stress, and pacing as these relate to intended meanings.
- Nonverbal language to include facial expressions, body language, gestures.
- Use and comprehension of figurative speech as a modifier of meaning.
- Comprehending the plot of a story, identifying subplots, conflicts, and resolutions in plots.
- Identifying relationships among the characters, the motivations, and development of a plot.
- Distinguishing between fantasy and reality, and appreciation of the effective uses of each to enhance dramatic quality.
- Using and analyzing persuasive language, stereotyping, propagandizing.
- Creative expression, role playing.
- Writing for specific purposes: to entertain, to persuade, to inform.

It can be readily seen that these aspects of traditional language arts programs are closely related to the development of critical viewing skills. Although critical viewing skills in the modern school program can be justified on their own merits, it should be reassuring to parents and educators to know that instruction in critical viewing skills actually restores certain long-neglected basic language skills to the curriculum.

In fact, in the case of skills that are appropriate to effective television viewing, which we refer to as receivership or critical viewing skills, it is necessary to ask whether these skills are not, in fact, part of the basic skills of the traditional language arts program. Although the case for the social value of TV viewing skills was clearly stated in the midfifties, it is relevant to direct attention to the nature of viewing skills as basic to the total language development of the individual. In fact, the traditional skills of language arts are served quite well by educational activities designed to enhance viewing skills.

The work done on critical viewing skills in the East Syracuse, New York School District provides examples of integration into the basic curriculum for purposes of social and intellectual development. At the sixth grade level, students are provided learning activities in identifying and analyzing the persuasive elements of TV commercials. Although this activity is integrated into an existing unit, *The Language of Symbols,* one of the expected outcomes is that the students will be more responsible consumers of goods and services.

This activity in critical viewing skills is preceded, in East Syracuse, by student work on advertisements in newspapers, magazines, and posters. A culminating activity has the students writing their own commercial scripts, using persuasive techniques for the purpose of selling their products. The esteemed basic skills of critical thinking are developed in this activity, which is concerned with making inferences from verbal and visual clues, separating fact from opinion, and developing criteria that can be used in evaluating persuasive messages in any medium.

In yet another critical viewing skills activity, the East Syracuse program combines the literary analysis of soap operas (plot, characterizations, resolutions) with the identification of content that uses sexist and ethnic stereotyping as sources of humor. The skills that are involved are neither new nor nonessential, but the advent of television has given them a new sense of relevancy. The program content provides the timely material that makes integration into the basic curriculum a natural development.

The writing of reviews of popular television shows has proven to be an assignment that uses critical viewing skills as the basis for writing. Students must deal with elements of plot, setting, time, characterizations, motivation, and resolution as they prepare to write a TV program review. The content of this intellectual exercise is analogous to the task of writing a traditional book report; where the major educational objectives deal with literary analysis and writing, the use of TV content provides a viable option.

A number of different responses have been formulated to deal with the threat many individuals and groups believe television holds for young viewers. In some schools there are programs aimed at reducing the amount of time children spend watching television. A major network has developed a program aimed at encouraging children to read more by involving them in reading the scripts of certain television programs. Yet other developments, such as Prime Time Television, provide guidance to teachers who would use television programs to supplement and enhance specific aspects of the regular instructional program. These developments have goals and objectives different from those of critical viewing skills programs.

It is important to note that critical viewing skills programs are not directed toward less viewing and more reading, as these do not represent their major purposes, which are to enable students to use television in a critical, discriminating manner. Just as it is inappropriate that teachers justify the development of composition skills on the grounds that it will lead students to become better spellers, so it is inappropriate to justify critical viewing skills because some children may be induced to read more or view less television.

THOUGHTS ON THE NATURE OF
TELEVISION AND ITS EFFECTS

Television has indeed filled a void in the communication needs of industrialized societies rapidly and intensively, but not without criticism. There has been an outpouring of concern over content portraying violence, content presenting sex, content touting products and political candidates, content purporting to be news or information. The objective of most of this criticism has been to change television, to bring it into line with what one special interest group or another thinks it should be. In general, these groups have failed to achieve their goals of control because they did not grasp that the fundamental nature of television is the same as the fundamental nature of all mass media — a means of expression for all the competing values, issues, needs, and desires that reside within our culture.

We — a people belonging to a culture with a set of shared values, rules of behaving with common symbols for understanding the world that surrounds us — are in a continual process of negotiating our culture. That negotiation gets done in the meeting rooms of our clubs, in the halls of our churches, in the living rooms of our homes, and in the content of our media. The contemporary content of our media provides the panoply of conflicts, offers, and counteroffers that the current negotiations involve. The contemporary content of our media, therefore, is not trivial. It is composed of the shared values, ideas, and symbols by which we survive as a people. As Cohn notes, "Television is a rich archive filled with primary source materials for the study of American society."

The media present us in reflection, distorted to be sure, but still recognizably us. Television and the other mass media are not adversaries of our culture; they are a part of it. Television does not change our culture; it confirms it by giving it expression. We as receivers are left to pick and choose from the whole array of views without guidance or restriction by the medium.

Given that media content is value laden and presented without guidance, what are the consequences when the values and ideas expressed are different from, or even in conflict with, those of members of the audience? Certainly, modern theoretical perspectives on the mass media have moved away from the concept of the all-powerful media holding in their hypnotic glow the lives of each and every one of us. Television, newspapers, magazines, and the cinema are parts of everyday life, as are indoor plumbing, the automobile, and inflation. Each affects the way we think, value things, and behave. However, each of these influences is managed by the individual for the purposes he or she chooses. In the normal circumstance, television and the media do not do things *to* people; people do things *with* the media. In the main, the effects of television and other media are those we seek out, those we choose to occur. The notion of personal management directs us away from the model of a passive receiver, out of control, who must be protected from the media, to the model of an active receiver, involved in the process of communication, who can learn skills of effectiveness.

Approaching the use of television, and media in general, as a process of personal management by an actively involved receiver will lead the critical viewing skills teacher away from directives, prescriptions, and proscriptions. Instead, the teacher will be well advised to help the students individually plan their management of the media. The next several sections of this chapter set out a scheme of ideas about how people make use of television and some instructional techniques to capitalize on those uses.

PEOPLE USING MEDIA

Scene One

"Hey, I'm home." The slam of the door left no doubt that indeed Melissa was home from another day of being a third grader. "What's to eat; I'm starving?" "Your snack is on the table, Lis." Melissa crossed to the kitchen, turned on the small TV set, and sat down to eat. A game show was in progress which she watched with little reaction. Her mother came into the kitchen and busied herself with some ever-present task. Melissa did little to acknowledge her presence. Some twenty minutes after she arrived home, Melissa pushed the plate away, turned off the TV, walked over to her mother and gave her a hug. "That was good, Mom." "Well, I'm glad you liked it. How was your day at school?" "It was OK. We did the neatest thing in reading today. It was about TV commercials. Did you know. . . ."

Melissa was part of a group of children who had kept a diary of their television viewing over a two-week period. When she shared her diary with us, we were intrigued by the regular pattern of the set going on at about 3:15 and off before 4:00. As we talked with her, the pattern of behavior, described in the scenario above, emerged. We asked her what she watched. "Whatever is on," she replied. We asked her why she watched TV. "To keep me company while I eat." We talked to her mother, who told us that such was the usual ritual when Melissa came home, and that by waiting for her to finish her snack before talking to her, she found Melissa much more interested in conversing about her day.

Scene Two

Each weekday afternoon at 5:00 the doorbell rang, followed immediately by an impatient knock. "That's got to be Eric; right on time," she said as she got up to answer the door. "Come on in; Amy and Eden are already downstairs with Angela." Eric, the four-year-old, next-door-neighbor, was dressed, as always, with an apron around his shoulders for a cape, vinyl cowboy boots and his gun belt wrapped twice around his shorts. He was dressed as his favorite superhero; it was time to watch the show.

Eric joined the three children downstairs. After watching for a few minutes they began to act out part of the scene they were watching. The television became a backdrop for their own play activity. When a particularly exciting scene came on, they would stop to watch and then go back to play. The television show was over long before the playing stopped.

Scene Three

John Roberts quickly flipped the bicycle over and stood it on the seat and handle bars. He was hurrying now because it was already after 8:00. He loosened the bolts on the back wheel and pulled it off the bike. He grabbed the tube repair kit and the pump and hurried into the house. "We'll be ready with half-time highlights of yesterday's games in just one minute," the television set announced. "Just made it," he thought.

Roberts felt pretty pleased with himself. Since dinner he had gotten the last of the fall cabbage picked, got some leaves raked, and was now ready to fix his young son's tire — all in time for the favorite part of the weekly nighttime football game. As the highlights came on, he watched intently. There had been quite a bit of talk at work about one of the Sunday games. He wanted to see the disputed call, as it was sure to engender even more discussion. The highlights over, the second half started. Roberts worked on the tire during the commercial breaks and when there was little action on the field. The instant replay made sure he'd have plenty of chance to see any excitement.

These three scenes exemplify three very different uses of television, conditions of viewing, and sources of satisfaction. Televiewing has long passed the novelty stage and is now woven into a fabric of most Americans' daily lives. Television has been successful, as all mass media, because it can serve a large number of different purposes. It is neither specialized nor demanding. If we could peer into the homes of some 60 million viewers, we would find nearly that many reasons for viewing. Here is a woman filling time waiting for her husband to finish getting ready to go out. Here is another deeply engrossed in some continuing drama. Here is a worker letting himself relax before bed. Here are two children pretending to be involved in a program to avoid going to bed. All of these viewers may be watching the same program. Each comes to view with a particular set of motivations and receptivity. The consequences of viewing will vary directly with those differing motivational and receptivity states. The understandings they gain and the satisfactions they draw from viewing may be substantially different. Content of a program is not a good predictor of the effects of viewing.

The notion that the same content can produce different effects in different people is older than the biblical parable of the sower of seeds; nevertheless, we have a long history in education and social science of expecting common and consistent effects across a group of persons, or a class, when we present common material to them. In the classroom, of course, teachers work to develop common motivations in order to obtain at least some consistency in result. In the individual viewing situation, there are few opportunities to develop common purposes. Each child's viewing, then, is highly individualistic. Consider the following scenario drawn from a lesson presented on *Sesame Street:*

This lesson was apparently designed to point out how important friends are to one's happiness. The principal characters in the segment were the puppets Bert and Ernie and the real-life person Maureen. The segment begins with Bert and Ernie arguing about the rights to a cookie that is in Ernie's possession. To prevent Bert from getting any, Ernie quickly eats the cookie; whereupon Bert informs Ernie that he will never speak to him again and pokes Ernie in the stomach. Because of the disagreement, they decide to terminate their friendship and pursue lives as far apart from each other as possible — one chooses the North Pole; the other will become a cowboy. Maureen enters and points out how empty and lonely their lives will be without one another. Bert feels guilty and apologizes to

Ernie for his aggressive behavior. Ernie reminds Bert that he was positive that the cookie was his. Bert asks Ernie how he can be so sure, to which Ernie counters, "Because I ate yours this morning."

The nature of this scene can generate a large number of interpretations and consequent effects. One child may key in on how clever Ernie is. Not only did he get both cookies, but he also got away with it with little more than an argument. This child's own experience with friends or siblings might reinforce that view, and consequently, the lesson will simply help maintain that behavior.

Another child might focus on the lesson that Bert might have learned. This child may perceive that people seldom really care about one another and consequently may find the final exchange where Ernie admits having eaten Bert's cookie earlier in the day to be entirely consistent with behavior or incidents he has observed.

Finally, a third child may perceive the segment exactly as intended — that indeed people are more important than possessions and that one should not be willing to abandon a friendship because of a dispute over a material object, however important at the moment. Because of the child's situational and psychological condition at the time, the content may even be perceived to have a great deal of application to her own behavior. The scenario demonstrates that content may be prosocial in intent and nature, but the applications by the viewers may not. The interpretations and consequences of viewing depend on the circumstances of the viewers, not on the content of the program. All of this is to say that one's motives for viewing are a key to understanding the consequences of attending to television.

THE MOTIVES OF HUMAN BEHAVIOR

Each of us is a composite of inborn traits and culturally determined characteristics. It is these traits and characteristics that provide for the regularity of our behavior. Our behavior is what identifies us as a person. The regularity of that behavior makes us knowable, predictable, and expresses our personality. Social scientists spend their careers studying the regularities, the patterns, of human behavior. Each of us in our daily dealings with one another make predictions based on our own study of the patterns of those with whom we interact. The sources of that regularity have been given a variety of names by social scientists. They are the primary and secondary drives, needs, instincts, values, beliefs, and so on that have appeared in the literature. For our purposes we can use the single term motivations.[1] Our motivations are the product of our birthright and the enculturalization process that each of us went through in becoming full-fledged members of our society. These motives are involved in everything we do. They are the source of our activity; they establish the scope of our behavior and the conditions of reward. These motivations are the hunger we feel at lunch; the need we have for social contact and approval; the fact that we breathe, need rest, do our job each day. Our motives and their behavioral expressions are, in fact, who we are.

Motives and Behavior

As we look over a class of children, we see the effects of a kaleidoscope of motives. A child who missed breakfast is jittery at his desk; another who stayed up too late has her head down. The class clown craves group approval, and the "good" little kid in the back just wants a smile from teacher. Each child's behavior is greatly shaped by the relative dominance of his motivations. As time and cycles progress, the picture changes. In the middle of it all, the teacher, too, experiences redirection of her behavior as her own motives ascend and decline. Every minute of every day this wondrous process occurs.

Analysis of Behavior in its Motivational Context

Question: When is the same behavior different? Answer: When it is evoked by a different motivational set. In producing the "same" behavior for different reasons, an individual focuses on different elements of the activity and establishes different expectations for its outcome. In watching television to become sleepy rather than, say, for information, program selection and involvement with content will be different, because the results that the individual is trying to achieve are different. Our motives for using television establish both

---

[1]As with all such notions, it is well to remember that motivation categories are conceptual devices, which help organize our thinking about human behavior. They are not necessarily real, but they approximate the processes we observe and permit us to talk about those processes.

the use itself and the gratification expected from that use. Because the use and gratification are specific to the motivational state, the consequences of viewing will change as the reasons for viewing change.

Let us return to each of the three scenes that began this section and attempt to interpret the use, gratifications, and consequences of each occasion of viewing.

For Melissa, televiewing was a transitional device as she made the change from the intense, highly social circumstances of school to the more intimate, interpersonal relations at home. She needed a period of time with an activity that restricted contact with others and at the same time provided a highly predictable, secure environment. Afternoon game shows make little demand on the viewer, and watching television does restrict other interpersonal contact.

For Eric, televiewing was part of the circumstances for social interaction with his peer group. At his age, Eric would be very unlikely to sit as an adult just to watch the superhero program. The program was a device around which play could be generated, much like going to a football game, playing cards, or other "adult" activities.

John Roberts' motives are more complex. Task completion is a very high need. Roberts would be uncomfortable sitting for an extended period "just watching television." However, doing two things at once is evidence of good planning and efficiency, a double reward. At the same time, he derives enjoyment from a particular content. Perhaps he was a successful player as a youth, and he can vicariously relive those successes in watching. Further, the content will provide him with a method of interaction with his lunch group. He will have a shared experience that will increase his sense of group membership and will enable him to contribute directly to the group's activity. Roberts would exhibit high commitment to the televiewing activity because it supplies a broad spectrum of gratification. Should his wife or family suggest turning the channel, a hostile response would likely result, although other circumstances might bring an agreeable response.

Let us consider three potential consequences of televiewing — retention of information, attitude change, and value formation — and consider the likelihood of each in the three viewing circumstances.

In Melissa's case, content is irrelevant to her purpose of watching. We would expect little or no retention. For the same reason, we would expect no effect on value formation. Attitudes toward her environment will change as she adapts herself to her new circumstances, but the change will not be a function of the TV program content that she viewed. The viewing simply maintains the conditions for the change to occur.

Eric is particularly susceptible to value formation because the circumstances of viewing provides direct, interpersonal reinforcement of certain activity values. Aggression as a solution may be encouraged. For the same reasons, attitudes might also be formed. Retention of content would be unlikely because there is no subsequent use expected on Eric's part. Note that television is an instrument for value formation and attitude development because it is functioning as an element within peer group interaction. It is, of course, this peer group interaction that supplies the real force behind any value or attitude developments.

John Roberts has selected the content and the conditions of viewing *because* of his attitudes and values. As an adult, changes in attitude or values are rare and usually involve cataclysmic occurrences, not common to television. We would expect Roberts to have high retention of the highlights and the incidents of the game because of the subsequent use at lunch time. Roberts may hold a position of an expert within his group on some aspect of football (e.g. refereeing). In this case he would be attentive to the aspect of the game and would be expected to be able to report in detail.

Developmental State

Focus and interpretation differences occur regularly between individuals and within individuals over time as motives shift. Differences also occur between and within individuals because of differences and changes in developmental state. Children and adults do not view television in the same way. Children in lower elementary grades are more likely to see a program as a series of quasi-independent events between which there may or may not be a connection. Listening to a child retell a story is much like viewing the scenery from a traveling car: there is a mountain; there is a river. The characters did this, and then they did that. The causal connectors are missing. The young child, therefore, lacks the perspective of the total story.

Children also show differences because of language development. While the structure and vocabulary used on television is neither technical nor highly complex, it is sufficiently advanced that children will miss the subtleties of explanation for the behaviors they see. There is little question that for children the actions do speak louder than words. Verbal humor with its rich referencing of cultural, historical, and contemporary events is often missed by children. Children prefer broad, slap-stick humor. Children may miss the double entendre, but they understand the leer.

Children are considerably less developed in their ability to process nonverbal, visual and auditory, information. For example, third graders typically do not practice visual conservation. That is, when an object changes size in screen image because it moves closer to the lens, many younger children perceive that the object has *grown* larger. Toys in close-up look larger and perhaps more attractive. Visual and auditory cues of perspective and size as presented on a two-dimensional screen and a single-direction audio source have to be learned. The symbols and signs of nonverbal language of which acting is so much a part must also be learned, although children are typically more advanced in this area than in verbal language.

CONTENT, CONSEQUENCES, AND THE CLASSROOM

To this point we have been looking at the uses of, and the gratifications from, televiewing from the perspective of the individual. Because most of our classroom instruction occurs in a group situation, it is worthwhile to consider the group perspective. The model used to explain individual viewing indicated that the reasons for the consequences of viewing are dependent on the particular set of dominant motives at the time of viewing. Viewing is initiated within the individual and its termination is determined by the gratification obtained by the individual. During the process of viewing, the reasons for viewing can change. This would result in changes in the perception of the content and the consequences of viewing. This conceptualization predicts strong individual differences in the way people use television, in the content that they see, in what they like, and in the subsequent uses that occur. In short, in a class of twenty-seven students, one can expect twenty-seven different explanations for viewing.

One way of looking at this notion is described in a wheel model.[2] To develop this model, consider an entire class encompassed in a circle. Each member of this class is a potential receiver of a television program. Given a particular television program, each member receives some portion of the content (for some, zero percent) and perceives that content according to the specific motivational conditions under which the individual is then operating. The perception of each individual is, in essence, unique but contains elements common to the perceptions of others in the audience. The degree of "commonness" or communality varies among pairs of class members and in most cases it varies widely. The behavioral responses produced subsequent to viewing by the class members will also vary widely because most mediated messages do not demand specific responses or do not have sufficient power to back up those demands. The perception of what the message is will vary as individual motives vary.

In the center of the circle, place a smaller circle or a hub that contains the content and situational variables. In research studies, it is these variables that are manipulated, controlled, or simply identified by the research. Every behavior subsequent to the presentation of the content can now be identified by spokes (radii) moving from the hub to the circumference of the circle. If we considered every aspect, each response would be unique. Consequently, the first wheel that we would draw would have twenty-seven spokes dividing the circle into twenty-seven equal arc segments. Each segment would represent the response of one person in the class. (*see* Figure 1.)

The model drawn gives us an accurate picture of the actual results one would expect from a given bit of television content and emphasizes that content is a poor predictor of subsequent audience behavior. Nevertheless, this model is not very useful for instructional purposes. To increase the instructional utility, we need to look for common elements among the unique responses. That is, some responses will be *functionally* the same. "Functionally the same" means that the consequences of the responses will be the same for

---

[2]The authors wish to acknowledge the contribution of Professors Timothy Meyer and Thomas Donohue to this section.

some other person or some other thing. Without developing a technical argument, the important concept here is that it is not the nature of the response that determines functional communality, but the method of classification that we use.

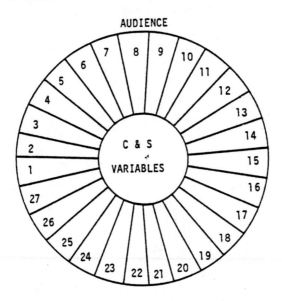

Figure 1.

The Content-Free, Content-Bound Wheel of Viewing

One very useful classification system for responses to televised messages is to identify them as content-bound or content-free. Content-free uses of television occur when the individual can use any content for the purpose he has. The earlier example of Melissa's use of television is a content-free use. Others might be using television to avoid going to bed or doing some chore; watching while waiting for someone; filling time; "cooling-off" in preparation for going to sleep.

On the other hand, little Eric's and big John Roberts' use of television were content-bound. Content-bound uses vary in the tightness to which they are bound to specific content. While a game show would not "work" for Eric's needs, any superhero type would. For Roberts, *the* football game is the only program that would be suitable. More general content-bound situations might be wanting to watch comedy after a particularly trying day; watching the news; turning on a morning "wake-up" show; watching cartoons on Saturday morning. The most specific content-bound situation is, of course, watching one's favorite program. A favorite program — not just the least objectionable program but one in which reasonable commitment and effort to watch is made — can be the source of insight into one's taste and needs. A discussion of favorites would be quite useful.

Returning to the class of twenty-seven students and the wheel model, we can now draw a wheel, using three categories. By selecting a viewing hour — say 8:00 P.M. — and having the children identify their viewing, the responses can be distributed into not viewing, content-free, and content-bound categories. Presume ten children were not watching; four children always watch television in the evening; three were watching what the rest of the family had chosen; another was avoiding the dishes; three had nothing else to do; two were watching their favorite program; three picked the program to watch for various reasons; and the last really liked the leading character. The wheel that represents this distribution would look like Figure 2.

The ten children who were not watching television at the 8:00 hour have been represented by the arc entitled "not viewing." The content-free section contains those who always view in the evening, those who were watching what someone else had chosen, and those who were avoiding or had nothing else to do. Note that some guesses had to be made here. We assumed that those who consistently watch at 8:00 probably derive their satisfactions from sources other than the content. That is, the time period is more important than the program. When one regularly watches at a particular time regardless of content, he may be seeking a secure, comfortable environment with few surprises or challenges. Relaxation of this sort is an important aspect of one's physical and psychic well-being. It should be a part of one's life and should be enjoyable without guilt.

The family viewing circumstance is another example where we have guessed that the gratifications from the social contact outweigh those from the specific content. Many families use the television set as a focal point for interaction, just as others might use a game board, cards, or a fire in the fireplace. Each of these provide a

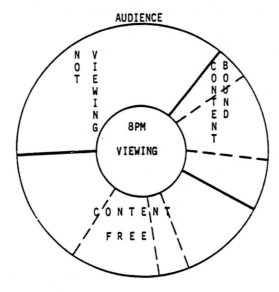

Figure 2.

common basis of experience, which can be shared by members of the group. The fact that a father can share a football game with his daughter and promote a firm relationship by doing it attests to the diversity of uses that a particular content can be put.

Those who explain their viewing by indicating they had nothing else to do have chosen television because of its availability rather than its content. This condition of viewing is, perhaps, the most troublesome to social thinkers. The viewer arrives at the set frustrated because of the lack of other activity. A precondition has been met that can lead to negative consequences. The problem is not the occasional occurrence but the night-after-night viewing to fill time, to meet the demand for something to do. It is neither the number of occasions nor the duration of televiewing that is important, *but the conditions under which the televiewing occurs.* The child who views night after night in the comfort of his family in the process of close, familial interactions experiences substantial positive outcomes. The child who views for the same period because no alternatives are present garners little gratification.

Our lone procrastinator may be enjoying the game of manipulation. Perhaps someone else will decide that the effort to get the televiewer back to the sink is greater than that required to do the dishes. At this point, the viewer has won the game. In our family observation studies, we often see children who practice such games. The acting is remarkable, and most of the actors can fully describe the techniques they use.

We have placed the remaining students in the content-bound category. Within this category there is still a wide variety of reasons for watching. Only two students are watching their favorite program; three are watching because they enjoy the program type (comedy, action/drama); and another because of a particular actor. Explorations of the gratifications received from this content will help the child understand some of the needs that shape his/her behavior.   .

Other Wheels of Viewing

Wheels can be built with any number of category schemes. Each one can have a particular instructional objective. In general the wheels sensitize the students to the conditions and consequences of viewing. Consequently, the child is able to make better use of this resource. Some examples of other categories follow: (1) Identify the actions subsequent to viewing. Take a specific hour of viewing and have the students indicate what they did *after* that hour — more viewing, play, homework, etc. (2) Record emotional change. Again take an hour of viewing. Have the children report how they felt on a positive/negative continuum before the hour of viewing and after the hour of viewing, then classify according to no change, positive change, and negative change. (3) Specify energy change. Use the same method as for emotional change.

Using a variety of category schemes helps the child realize that behavior of any sort has multiple consequences in what one does or how one feels.

TELEVISION AS STORYTELLER

In this brief reflection on children and television, it may be helpful to consider the very important role that has been played by nonprint communication in the socialization process, a role that appears to have been recently assigned to television. Storytelling was, for thousands of years, the means whereby the important information about living was communicated to the young, an oral tradition that is to this day practiced by some major religious groups. The stories that were told from the earliest human beginnings were of three principal types.[3] The stories that showed *how things worked* sought to visualize and exemplify the most important aspects of life that involved man's relation to other humans and man's relation to the natural environment. Such stories were largely based on fiction and myth, often highly dramatized.

Another kind of story dealt with *what things are*, and through legend and more recent accounts of experience, attempted to present a factual report to the neophytes of the tribe. Hence, the young would learn about the nature of lightning, the secrets of the sea, the origins of the winds, and other phenomena and events.

Finally, there were stories that dealt with *values and choices*, the vehicles for conveying the moral and ethical verities of the tribe. Through such stories, the young would learn the values of loyalty, honesty, and charity, especially when applied to one's own people.

It is generally recognized that the telling of these kinds of stories was an essential factor in the socializing process in all human groups, and that such storytelling continues to fill an important role today, although the storytellers may have changed considerably (it is well to remind ourselves of the oral "storytelling" traditions that still bring people together for important religious observances — holidays, weddings, christenings, funerals, to name the more obvious).

With the coming of the printing press, industrialized societies, and mass education outside of the home, the institution of storytelling was greatly altered. In fact, it disappeared in its older intimate form where trusted members of family and tribe were the storytellers. In Gerbner's view, the factual lessons of the school replaced the *what things are* stories and the *how things work* stories were taken over by the specialists of various arts, crafts, vocations, and professions. The stories about *values and choices* seem to be shared by religious figures, counselors, and the newspaper advice columnists.

It is necessary to remember that the purposes for which stories are told have not changed from preliterate times to the present. Through the story, it has been possible for man to come into contact

---

[3]George Gerbner, Dean of the Annenberg School of Communications, University of Pennsylvania, developed these points in an address to the First National Conference on Children and Television, in Philadelphia, Nov. 6, 1979.

with reality in an indirect manner. This phenomenon of human communication provides television with the potential to become quite as influential in the ritual of storytelling as was any old sage of the tribe.

It becomes evident that the concerns of many organizations, such as Action for Children's Television and the Parent Teachers Association, are more than protests against violence and sex in TV programming. In fact, the "moral alternative" groups of the early 1980s are fearful that the stories about how things work in life have been taken over by TV shows such as "Three's Company" and "One Day at a Time."

There has always been the requirement that a good story must be entertaining, whether it be tragedy or comedy. In the struggle to be the nation's number one storyteller, each network strives to ensure that the stories contained in its programming are entertaining, even though it may mean that conventional mores must be challenged.

Indeed, the American people have generally accepted television as their storyteller. As Gerbner has pointed out, television has become the most pervasive, universal, common socializing force in the national community. Television has become an institutionalized teller of life's stories, entertaining and ritualized for the vast majority of the people who engage in regular, nonselective viewing of its programs. Just as people have for decades sent their children to schools and churches for social processing, they now "turn on the tube" to be informed, entertained, persuaded, and sold by the new storytellers of the age of television.

It would be overstating the case to claim that television has replaced all other important storytellers of the time, but it is an inescapable fact that, by sheer amount of time spent in viewing, the "typical" American child has given television a lion's share of the action. The long-range implications of this transformation in the process of communication and socialization are probably more complex than contemporary critics of television recognize. Efforts to educate children for the effective uses of television must take into account the storytelling function of television.

INTEGRATING CRITICAL VIEWING
SKILLS INTO THE ON-GOING CURRICULUM

Inasmuch as the terms integration and correlation are so commonly used in discussions of curriculum matters, and not indiscriminately, it may be useful to consider, briefly, the integration of critical television viewing skills into the regular school program.

First, the major objectives of critical viewing skills instruction share a common psychological base with the major objectives of the language arts and with selected objectives of social studies. This condition is a requirement for the integration process. In other words, integration of a new element into a curriculum area can be done only where there is extensive compatibility between the objectives of the new curricular element and the existing curriculum area into which the new element will be integrated.

Comprehending the message is an objective that is pursued in the most traditional language arts programs and it is a major objective of critical viewing skills instruction. The integration of critical viewing skills instruction into the language arts program will strengthen that program, while it provides for the extension and application of skills to the new medium of television. Language skills are no longer restricted to print medium, to be sure, but it is expected that children who develop critical viewing skills will make concurrent gains in the applications of language skills to conventional material.

Integration, then, is feasible where the objectives of the existing program will not be replaced by the objectives of a new curriculum element, but where the existing objectives will provide a support base for the pursuit of the new program objectives.

The educational objectives of the new elements and existing programs must be analyzed to determine the extent of compatibility and mutual support, for it is these "intended pupil learnings" that will tell the story. If, for example, there is similarity between content rather than between "intended learning outcomes," then correlation would more likely be the appropriate way to proceed. We may relate the study of Colonial American Literature and Colonial American History and such studies may be scheduled concurrently, sometimes with the same teacher. Unless the specified educational objectives are common to both courses, there is a good case for correlation and little to justify attempts at integration.

With these comments regarding integration and correlation, it may be expected that the social studies area will lend itself to more limited integration of critical viewing skills than will the language arts. As students encounter the value and decision questions posed by television content, the social studies provide a logical ground for integration. Stereotyping, political images, consumerism, and environmental issues are examples of television program content that call for the use of critical viewing skills in the social studies curriculum field.

Chapter 2

BUILDING BASIC SKILLS
WITH TELEVISION COMMERCIALS

THE general concern expressed over the effects television commercials have on children has several dimensions. On the one hand, parents often complain that TV commercials which feature junk foods, toys, and games of questionable merit, and newly released movies, induce their children to bring pressure on parents to buy the item or service. Parents feel that their children have enough to do in dealing with peer pressures without being assaulted by appealing TV commercials.

Another concern is that the appeals used to sell products on television actually present a false picture of reality. The child viewer is told, in some TV commercials, that the possession of a certain game or toy will make him instantly popular with other children in the neighborhood. A junk food commercial suggests that every child who really has fun will eat "Tasty Tarts" after the game of kickball in the backyard.

Other complaints from parents and teachers stem from the confusion of genuine human needs with the transitory and faddish desires promoted by many commercials. Furthermore, the idea of setting buying priorities, of coping with the problems of infinite wants and limited resources, is seldom a part of TV commercials.

Fortunately, all of these concerns can be dealt with through the provision of learning experiences in critical viewing skills as part of language arts and social studies instruction. Let us identify important concepts from the social studies area that can be taught through the critical study of the TV commercials which most children see in their favorite programs.

1. Advertising is an important part of the competitive free enterprise system, as various companies seek to sell their products to large numbers of people.
2. When people have freedom of choice in spending their money, advertisers will attempt to influence the choices in favor of cer-

tain goods and services.

3. Most people do not have enough money to buy all the goods and services they would like, so they must make choices. Buying one thing may mean that they cannot buy another (buying an expensive boat may "cost you the opportunity" of buying a new automobile).

4. Since people have infinite wants and limited resources for buying, they must decide those goods and services that are most valuable, most gratifying, to them.

5. In the free enterprise system, the consumer (buyer) must be prepared to protect herself from misleading advertising.

These important concepts will provide young citizens with the foundation for understanding why TV commercials are part of "free" television in the United States. Somebody has to pay for the free programs that come from the networks and that somebody is the company that sponsors a program during which the company's commercials are shown.

Although there are many complaints about TV commercials, it is helpful to understand that they are part of the free enterprise market system. They may be annoying and they may be offensive and misleading on occasions, but they are a part of the system that encourages competitive enterprise and freedom of choice by the consumer. Through education, the American consumer prepares to become a wise and discriminating buyer.

In order to provide a rich information resource to your students as they gain skill in analyzing TV commercials, you will need to know quite a bit about this topic. Fortunately, the technical side of commercials is not too difficult for most teachers who have grown up since the beginning of the TV era. You will probably think of many examples from your own viewing that will "fit" the analytical discussion here.

Before we deal with educational objectives and learning experiences for children, let us have a "few words about commercials." As we consider TV commercials, we will find ourselves learning about "how things work," "what things are," and "values and choices," as these traditional types of stories are told in TV commercials.

American commercial television is based on the notion of circulation, which means that program decisions are made in terms of the number of noses that are pointed toward the screen. It is these "noses" that the advertiser buys when buying commercial time on a station or network. Once the audience has been delivered into their hands, the advertisers respond with a commercial message on which they have likely spent more than $50,000. Every element of the message has been created for its capacity to influence the viewers to buy a product or service.

It is the "intent to sell" that is the primary distinguishing characteristic of the TV commercial. It is this characteristic that must be understood in order to place the content into its proper perspective. Phrases such as "helps get your teeth their whitest" are subject to multiple interpretations. Further, if we assume that all toothpaste products help get teeth their whitest in some way or another, the phrase provides no reason for the purchase of this brand. Advocacy language in the United States (whether it be advertisements, legal briefs, or policy statements) has a firm tradition which holds that while it is not permissible to lie, it is also not necessary to tell the whole, unvarnished truth. The notion is the concept of "puffery." This term was defined by the U.S. Supreme Court early in our business history as permissible aggrandizement of the qualities of a product one wishes to sell. It is permissible because it is the common expectation of the market place that the seller will participate in such practices; consequently, no reasonable buyer will be taken in.

It is not necessary to take the position that children are ignorant lambs in the market place. Children typically show themselves to be capable of making market decisions to select the products that meet their needs. Their criteria may not always agree with ours, but their criteria are usually justified. In short, a child may select candy over spinach, but she does so on the basis of taste, smell, texture, appearance and so forth, not on the basis of a commercial alone. Clearly, however, there are circumstances in which a child's limited experience may lead him to be more susceptible to the blandishments of commercial advertising. To explain those conditions, let us first look at how commercials work.

COMMERCIALS EXPLOIT HUMAN NEEDS; THEY DO NOT CREATE NEEDS

Each decision that we make is somehow a combination of our physical needs, our social requirements, and the life-styles of our family and community. Our bodies require nourishment, but our culture establishes the conditions under which we will eat — three meals a day with fork and spoon (or chopsticks) etc., and even what we will eat (fried ants are not yet in great demand). We have established an elaborate social structure to provide our nourishment. We have the occupations of farmer, processor, trucker, grocer, and so forth.

Our familial roles are still defined by those responsible for "bringing home the bacon" and those who serve it at the table. This process of eating, then, has established a large number of problems for which a number of products and services have been developed as solutions. Because we fry our foods, we need cooking oil; because we eat off of dishes, we need products to clean them; because being a good cook is part of being a good parent we have all the product "helpers," or a fast food chain to serve as our surrogate mother (they do it all for you). The point of this is that products and services respond to the physical and psychological requirements that are intrinsically part of us as members of the human race and members of a particular culture.

Commercials do not establish the need for status within our peer group. They may attempt to heighten the importance of status in order to raise the value of the product they tout, but status structures are fundamental. Sex appeal is a function of our culture, not of our toothpaste. We are all aware that an after shave lotion is not the *sine qua non* of love, but our modern superstitions appear to require it.

There is an apocryphal story of the anthropologist who asked the member of another culture if he really believed that his yams would walk away to his neighbor's field if they were not guarded each night. "Probably not," was the reply, "but I can't afford to take the chance." Many commercials play on the unknown or on situations too volatile to predict: I don't know if my carburetor is staying clean and so I buy additives for my gasoline.

The commercial writer begins with the fundamental drives, needs, desires, and sources of happiness of the human condition. She then attempts to associate the product or service with the satisfaction of those drives and needs, or with the occasion of happy outcomes. Typically, ads directed toward children emphasize the notion of having fun. With the exception of girls helping their mothers in the kitchen, children are rarely shown to be productive or helpful (boys apparently cannot be helpful) and to be getting satisfaction from it. Children need to understand that there are limits to fun-evoking activities and that "fun" may not be an adequate basis for making a buying decision, just as we need to understand that Brut® after shave is not what makes Joe Namath sexy. The child, then, is making his decisions on the same basis as the adult — on the promise that some good effect will occur.

PRODUCT EVALUATION — PERFORMANCE VERSUS PROMISE

Children and adults can evaluate a product on the basis of whether the performance of the product meets the promise that has been made by a commercial. There are at least three conditions that limit our ability to evaluate. (1) The product may be unknown to the buyer. In this circumstance the buyer has limited resources with which to decide. A careful cataloguing of product information produces a pitifully short list. Without knowing someone who makes use of the product in the same manner that we would, there are no commonly available information sources for most household products. When product information is available in magazines or newspapers, more likely than not it is based on a press release from the company and not on independent research (there are, of course, notable exceptions). Consequently, with a new or otherwise unknown product, the would-be buyer has little to go on but price and such ephemeral qualities as reputation, packaging, and the like.

(2) In the second limiting case, the performance promised may be difficult to measure. That gasoline additive may have nothing to do with the performance of one's car, but the car does perform properly. A deodorant promises social acceptance, and if one can still find people who will go to lunch with him, he may credit the deodorant. Are these products performing to their promise or is the person participating in a modern day superstition? Like the yam farmer, he has decided that it is cheaper and easier to continue a belief than to check it out.

(3) The extent of need limits one's ability to evaluate. If a certain automobile promises a status a person cannot get from other sources, she can find that status in that automobile simply because she has been told often enough that it does provide status. She wants

to believe that it is true, and her belief is sufficient. That is, she does not have to demonstrate its validity to anyone else. The stronger her need for status, and the greater the extent to which it is blocked, the more she will believe that that automobile will bring her status. Strong needs will invest great importance to potential solutions. Parents, at times, convince themselves that toys and other material possessions are expressions of love that substitute for time spent with their children; children learn this game rapidly and play on parent's guilt to score points by getting objects they will soon discard. We can learn about our society by asking which segments of it are susceptible to certain commercial appeals. Personal care products are primarily sold on the basis of social acceptance. Teenagers, and persons in highly competitive circumstances, are the primary users of such products. Social acceptance is a substantial concern to these groups.

COMMON SELLING TECHNIQUES
USED IN PRODUCT COMMERCIALS

The underlying requirement of successful advertising is quite simple — to show that the product or service will solve a problem or satisfy some need. The process by which this is accomplished can, of course, be complicated. There are, however, a relatively small number of advertising techniques, which accommodate the majority of selling approaches.

Product Qualities

One classification of advertisements includes those which demonstrate the qualities of the product. In these advertisements the need for the product is usually assumed (e.g. refrigerators, ranges, automobiles, etc.). Positive product qualities are displayed. Rarely are negative attributes mentioned, and if they are, it is usually to convince the buyer that the advertiser is honest.

Comparative advertising has increased in frequency in the last few years. Comparative advertising specifically identifies a competitor and shows how the qualities of the advertised product are more effective than the competing product. Again, only positive comparisons are provided. The wording of comparative advertising has become particularly complex as the writers attempt to limit the comparisons to those particular elements where an advantage can be claimed. For example, phrases like "For pain other than headache" or "These products contain aspirin and other ingredients you may not want" are important keys for the buyer, but they can easily be missed.

Whether dealing with straight description or with comparisons, what is *not* said about the product qualities is often more important than what is. The qualities that are not described may indicate areas of product weakness. Further, the wording of the descriptors that are used need not be precise. The phrase "Works up to twice as long" does not mean that it will and does not exclude the interpretation that it will work only "half as long." Of course, it may not tell you "as long as what."

Problem-Solution

When the need for a particular service or product is not well-established, advertisements will approach the selling situation in two steps: The first will establish a problem or need; in the second step the product will be shown as the solution. The problem: taking off your shoes in a Japanese restaurant; the solution: *Odor-Eater®* inserts. With sufficient examples of this nature the ad campaign can convince us that we all have a problem with foot-odor and prepare us to buy Odor-Eater as the product that will solve our problem.

Slice of Life

A variant of the problem solution approach is "Slice of Life." Slice of life dramatizes a common problem situation and presents the product as the solution. The new user is then typically shown receiving praise and admiration for being such a clever person. Many coffee commercials use this approach.

Association

Associative commercials attempt to establish a desirable mood in which the product is seen as a necessary part. The product may be associated with feminity, masculinity, love, good times, whatever.

Commercials that strive for acceptance by association depend on the viewer to make the connection. A product cannot directly promise "love" without running afoul of the Federal Trade Commission, but the product can be shown as an important element in relations involving love. Tooth paste and mouthwash commercials often use the association approach.

Identification

An extension of association is the identification approach. A common technique will make use of a person established in the public eye as the spokesperson for products that may be unrelated to the competence of the person. Pat Boone advertises a skin cleanser. Anita Bryant sells Florida orange juice. Identification works because the viewer wants to be like the commercial spokesperson or because the spokesperson is deemed credible because he maintains a positive public image, in spite of the fact that singers may have no special competence in cleansers or juices.

Competence

There are instances where persons competent in a field will endorse products related to that field. Every tennis racquet selling for over fifteen dollars seems to be signed by some tennis player. What does it mean to be "endorsed for championship play"? Identification is clearly functioning here, also; the difference is that the spokesperson has the additional credits of being successful professionally or in competition. An interesting example of the twists this approach can take shows Karl Malden, trading on the competence of a police character he played on television to tell us about stolen credit cards. The "Marcus Welby" character has been used in a similar way in commercials in which the good doctor assures us that Sanka® will help prevent frayed nerves.

Price

The last in this list of selling appeals is price. Reduce the price sufficiently and any product will sell. For some people, a bargain is irresistible regardless of product quality. Certain ball point pen commercials use the price appeal.

Combinations

Many commercials are obviously combinations of these techniques. Price can combine with any element; association and identification are often used together. The value of these classifications is not so much that they help us to choose the techniques of analysis but that we would use them to understand the message. Helping the child develop his own system does appear to have value in that it gives him an assimilated, short-hand method for identifying persuasive appeals in many kinds of messages.

TEACHING CHILDREN TO EVALUATE COMMERCIALS

There are five basic steps by which commercial messages can be evaluated. First, *identify what is promised explicitly and implicitly in both the audio and visual portions of the message.* Toothpaste ads explicitly promise white teeth and clean breath and implicitly promise that the user will be attractive to the opposite sex. Cola ads explicitly promise refreshment and implicitly promise sunny days, good friends, and good times. Certain automobile ads promise a macho life with status, sexual success, and adventure. This first step identifies what the individual is buying — the sources of satisfaction that are to be tapped by this product. One does not buy shampoo; one buys body, lustrous hair, loving glances, and social success. Promises are contained in practically each element of a well-made commercial. They are in the images evoked by the music. (One excellent teaching technique is to record the opening music, before the announcer begins, of a number of commercials, play this music to the class, and have them identify the kind of product that the music seems to fit.)

Spokespersons are chosen to express characteristics that can be associated with the product. Young, beautiful women are chosen to sell shampoo; sports heroes or character actors use their images to sell products with which we can identify. We can easily identify the selling characteristics by asking our students to substitute a spokesperson with differing characteristics. What would be your response to an elderly, white-haired woman selling Earth-Born® shampoo? Would your response change if the announcer's voice was high-pitched rather than low and masculine? What is successful about Karl Malden as a spokesman for American Express? Why is the character of Tony the Tiger friendly, deep-voiced, but not highly competent? Why is the promise in the Frosted Flakes® commercial love instead of nutrition?

The settings of a well-made commercial are selected for the images they evoke. Diaper commercials show neat, well-appointed rooms — the domain of a woman obviously in control; no unseemly clutter with a mother who uses Pampers®. Pepsi-Cola® is sold on a delightful beach or by an exquisite mountain stream. Headache pain is explored in stark simplicity; relief comes in much more pleasant surroundings.

As one explores commercials, certain characteristics emerge. Some commercials focus on a specific target audience with a specific, direct promise of a solution to a specific problem. Many over-the-counter drug commercials are of this type. Others will overlay the function of the product with images of other results, which may not be immediately connected with the product. Personal care products are of this type (she enjoys tennis more with mini-pads). Still others will not discuss the function of the product at all but will deal solely with broad promises related to self-image. Automobile ads are often of this sort.

One also learns that not every commercial is well crafted. In fact, quite a few are poorly made — a circumstance more likely with the commercials produced for local station use. These commercials are particularly useful in class as they permit the student to explore methods by which they could be improved.

Once the product performance promised by the commercial has been identified, the students are ready for the second step: *Identify the criteria by which the performance is to be evaluated.* Criteria for evaluation can come from two sources: the commercials themselves and from the buyers. Commercials will often express or imply the criteria by which the product should be evaluated in the manner in which the performance promise is expressed. We as buyers usually (but surprisingly not always) have overt or covert criteria for evaluation. For example, most women can express specific reasons for the use of a particular shampoo; most children cannot.

Criteria expressed in the commercial establish a set of ground rules under which the purchase is to be made. One toothpaste commercial asks, "But will it really get my teeth white?" To which the reply is given, "It gets my teeth their whitest" (this line is followed by a gleaming display of teeth one could suspect are capped and otherwise technically augmented). The line is an excellent example of indirection. The purchaser may be expected to reason that if the toothpaste gets her teeth white, it will get my teeth white. Again, the *persona*, in character, not in real life, is saying, "This product worked for me." For many of us, this statement from a credible person is sufficient to justify the purchase and continued use of a product. This same toothpaste commercial provides at least two other criteria for evaluation: One is in the smiles of the performers. The viewer is given a direct image of the results of use of the product. The second is in the reported success of the new user in recapturing a lost love.

The purchaser may or may not adopt the criteria expressed in the commercial. In spite of efforts by *Close Up*® to associate toothpaste with sex appeal, one may buy toothpaste on the basis of taste, fluoride, or price. Maintaining specific criteria makes one both less susceptible to some commercials and more susceptible to others. If my sole criterion is price, then ads that present the qualities of the product have little impact, but a sale ad may have an immediate effect. Typically, advertisements that tap directly into a problem perceived by the receiver have greater likelihood of effect, but only with those persons who feel they have that problem.

The third step in the evaluation process is, *determine whether the criteria are appropriate to the product or service.* Basically, this step investigates whether or not the effects or results that we seek from a product or service are reasonable expectations. Is it reasonable to expect a toy to give "hours of fun," or a detergent to get the wash "whiter than white," or a toothpaste to get my teeth as white as the smile on TV? In short, what can these products actually do? We need to direct the students to cut through the hyperbole of the commercial message to establish realistic criteria of performance.

Advertisements for products will often attempt to associate the product with the satisfaction of some basic need (status, love, etc.). This association may give rise to criteria or expectations very unlikely to be fulfilled. One method of determining the appropriateness of such criteria is to consider the function of the product. What is this product supposed to do? Toothpaste is made to clean teeth, a perfume to provide a lingering scent for some period of time, automobiles to provide transportation from one point to another. When we consider function, products become prosaic, perhaps explaining why so many products are not advertised on the basis of function.

Finally, there is a group of products whose functional performance is taken for granted and that is marketed on the basis of secondary characteristics. Facial soaps are good examples. The primary function of facial soaps is, of course, to aid in cleansing. However, most advertisements emphasize secondary attributes such as the perfume, shape, color, other ingredients such as deodorizers, lotions, etc. Is it reasonable to buy a soap because of its scent? Of course, particularly if it also performs its primary purpose. One only begins to wonder about the efficacy of buying decisions when they are consistently made on some basis for which the product has no capacity. To buy a breakfast cereal because sweet things mean love, to buy a perfume expecting romance, to change your toothpaste to recover a lost love, to beg for a toy to win neighborhood friends, all suggest attitudes with limited utility.

Getting children to examine motives beyond the most simple is quite difficult. The question "Why did you do that?" is too often used as a pejorative in prelude to punishment. One way that seems to work is to let children solve someone else's problem. A short little scenario — "John has just moved into a new neighborhood and is not having too much success in making friends. His birthday is coming up. What presents do you think he should ask for?" — might well serve the purpose of introducing the notion that people often buy things for purposes other than their primary function.

In considering the appropriateness of the motives we identify, we must be careful not to suggest that one set of motives is necessarily correct. People buy products and services to solve some need problem they may or may not be able to articulate. Satisfaction with a product or service comes from the solution of that problem. If one buys a baseball mitt autographed by a certain player hoping to gain acceptance by the team, and it works, then as far as the criteria of selection are concerned, they were fully appropriate. The process of determining appropriateness involves the process of determining the problem we are trying to solve. Consider that someone is buying a dishwashing detergent on a functional basis, that is, to get the dishes clean. The criterion of selection that the person is using is price. This criterion is appropriate only if one can assume that there are no differences in cleaning ability among products of different price. For the complete range of products, this assumption probably is not true. We may introduce a limiting condition to that range, however, if our budget will permit us to buy only detergents priced at 89¢ or lower. Under these conditions, the criterion of price is again appropriate.

Once the criteria of purchase and the problem to be solved have been established, we can move to the fourth step of evaluation: *Determine the likelihood of success of the product or service as a solution to the need problem.* This determination requires one to examine the product or service for the qualities that it can provide. If my best friend has lost interest in me, will changing the flavor of my toothpaste rekindle the flame? If I'm the new boy on the block, will a new bicycle help me win friends? How about a new swimming pool? Each of our need problems carries with it the conditions for its solution. What are the conditions for winning new friends? One has to meet them and have some basis for interaction over time to gain acceptance. Both a new bicycle and a new swimming pool may provide opportunities for those conditions.

The last step in this evaluation process is *establish the value of the performance of the product or service in terms of the individual.* Value increases as the need of the individual increases and as the number of alternative solutions decreases. The single solution to a high need state is very valuable to the individual. Valuation is clearly a very personal thing. It is compounded by the fact that each of us has limited resources to meet the various need states we have, in terms of time, capability, money, and so forth. Helping children value an activity involves an examination of the trade-offs involved, an increased understanding of alternatives, and an analysis of the consequences of each. Children often do not understand the notion of trade-offs or opportunity cost, the fact that doing one thing will preclude the doing of something else. It is helpful to teach this concept first as it is a factor in many elements in the use of media, including the selection of programs to watch.

This five step evaluation process involves a dual understanding. We may be initially concerned with an understanding of the commercial message. What is its intent and many elements? Ultimately we have to understand ourselves to understand what impact the message may have on us. Most commercial messages are irrelevant to most television viewers. Advertisers estimate that a message may have impact on about 3 percent of the audience. Advertisements directed toward a solution of a need problem for which the viewing individual already has found an adequate solution will essentially be ignored. Should the individual be dissatisfied with his present solution, or should he lack a solution, advertisements that link a product to a promised solution will have passed the initial condition for getting the attention of the viewer. This precondition, of course, does not guarantee selling impact. The arguments and images presented may not be convincing. The person may become distracted if the commercial is poorly made. But, if the message has tapped a need state, the advertiser has found a necessary key to whatever consequences follow.

BRAND NAMES, PACKAGING, AND THE SUPERMARKET

Charles is in the family room watching his favorite superhero on the afternoon show. "You never outgrow your need for milk," the announcer intones. "And when you buy your milk, make sure it's Quality Checked!"

"Charles," his mother calls, "I need you to go down to the store for me. Here is a list of the things I want you to buy. The money is on the table."

"Aw, Mom, this is my favorite show."

"Come on, Charles, I need this done now."

Charles starts off, still grumbling to himself a bit, but actually, a trip to the store, on his own, is kind of neat, especially since he bargained an extra twenty cents for his trouble.

"OK, first on the list is bread," he thinks, half aloud. "What is that kind I like? Oh, here it is; it has that gold band around the middle. Now milk. My gosh, look at all these different kinds of milk. Mom likes that skinny kind and *no glass bottles*. I broke the last one. Oh, here we go; Quality Checked, that's a good kind. And the last thing is lettuce. Boy, just three things. What did I need this dumb list for? I could remember three things. Sure is a lot of lettuce here. Mom always squeezes these things. Bet this one's ripe, it feels nice and soft. Well, I got my list. Now for my treat. I guess I'll get some gum. . . . Really like a candy bar, but its too close to dinner, blah.

It's gotta be sugarless. I like that TriFree kind. I wonder where they keep it. Excuse me," he said out loud to the man stocking vegetables. "Where do you keep the TriFree gum?"

"Oh, that's up front by the cash registers. The TriFree is on the left. Say, are you getting the lettuce for your mom?"

"Yeah"

"Well, let me show you something. . . ."

Brand Names

The supermarket, and self-service stores generally, have brought about a tremendous change in the marketing strategies of many goods. As we push our way up the aisle, we are faced with a fantastic array of products and brands within products. Each notation on our list is a decision point. No longer can we rely on the advice of a trusted sales person. We must rely on our own experience, memory, and impulse. In many cases, we have established through experience a brand name product we always buy. In others, we buy on a price per unit basis, and if price is the same, then our selection is on convenience of packaging or color or some other superficial reason.

A great deal of television advertising is directed toward our supermarket shopping routines. One purpose of advertising is to establish the brand name of a product. Brand names do more than just identify a particular manufacturer of a product. Each brand name is a shorthand notation for the qualities that the product is supposed to embody. This technique is called positioning. Positioning attempts to establish a brand as THE brand for a particular purpose. Hence, Crest® is the cavity fighter toothpaste; Close-up® is for fresh breath and white teeth; and so on. If, in the advertising campaign, the advertiser can get the viewer to remember the brand name and its positioning labels, the product will have an edge at the point of purchase.

Consider Charles and the purchase of the milk. He did not have a brand name to immediately direct his purchase. He did have two limiting characteristics — low-fat and paper or plastic cartons. Within those limits, however, there was still a range of choice. What directed his decision was the familiarity with a phrase, Quality Checked. That phrase positioned that brand as a choice that would be approved of at home.

When we are faced with a decision among choices of approximately the same value, we search for information that will reduce the uncertainty and risk of the decision. Advertisers attempt to make use of that behavior by providing any possible note of familiarity at the point of purchase.

We can raise the consciousness of our students to this attempt by simple word and symbol association games. The phrase "All Tempa____" should bring an immediate response — *Cheer*®. The sight of Mr. Whipple should direct other images. Familiarity is an important basis on which to make judgments, but we need to interrogate the source of that familiarity to be sure that it is an adequate one on which to base the decision.

Brand names also point out that a manufacturer may produce the same product under many slightly different forms. *Crest*®, *Gleem*®, and *Gleem II*® are three toothpastes all made by the same company, Proctor and Gamble. Proctor and Gamble, Lever Brothers, American Home Products, and other large companies all make several brands of the same product because (1) consumers buy the same product for different reasons, and it's easier to position a brand name with only one or two qualities rather than several qualities; and (2) when the consumer buys a product on the basis of an advertising promise that it doesn't keep, brand dissatisfaction occurs, and a brand shift is likely. As most household products are advertised with an underlying association with fundamental qualities which the product cannot functionally provide (Jell-O® still cannot guarantee a happy marriage), consumer turnover is a constant effect. So, the large companies have another brand available when you tire of their first offering.

Packaging

Innovative packaging can be a distinct product quality. A salad dressing with a shaker top, which restricts the flow, might be a plus for a shopper with children at home. Packaging also provides the advertiser with several additional opportunities to tip the decision scale in her favor. A particular shape, design, or color may provide information or tap into cultural beliefs. Our advertising friends tell us of a study in which three boxes of detergent were put to a consumer test. One was yellow, one red, and the third blue. Although the test consumers were led to believe otherwise, the detergent inside all three boxes was the same. The respondents used the detergents for a month. Their report: The detergent in the red box was too strong, the detergent in the yellow box too weak, but the detergent in the blue box was just right in strength. How many blue detergents can you think of?

The word "natural" is in current vogue. We'll find it in prominent display on a variety of packages. Packagers have begun to respond to the worries about additives by adding descriptive phrases like "To aid in mixing" to explain poly-syllabic chemical names that grandma never knew.

Finally, distinctive packaging helps the consumer find the product on the shelf. A poor package does not compete for your attention. It does no good to position a brand name if the consumer cannot find it at the store. Sometimes you will see different brands evolve toward similar packaging as the less successful brands begin to adopt the shape and style of the more successful ones. It is worth it to the manufacturer if he can sell even 10 percent of his product on the basis of a selection error that you make at the point of purchase.

Supermarkets

There have been a number of guides on how to shop at supermarkets: always use a list; do not go when you are hungry; avoid impulse buying. Beyond shopping, the supermarket and other self-service stores are prime sources of product information. Conveniently displayed before you are several brands of the same product and several products of the same use class. There is little better opportunity to compare ingredients, packaging, size, use recommendations, price, etc. in order to improve your buying decisions. A field trip to the supermarket with adequate planning and parental support, timely notification of store personnel and their cooperation can be an important part of helping children learn about the tasks of wise consumerism.

Good techniques of product evaluation are a necessity if viewers are to properly assess the information provided in television commercials.

THE IMPORTANCE OF THE TV PRODUCT COMMERCIAL

Television commercials are part of the advertising keystone to a free enterprise system. Free enterprise, where the market establishes the standards of quality, price, variety, and use, can only function if the consumer has an adequate opportunity to be informed about the products of the marketplace. It is the manufacturer's responsibility to provide this information if his product is to survive, for no one is better suited to tell us about a product than the manufacturer himself. Television with its wide appeal has become an important source of product information.

Television commercials also provide the economic basis for our commercial television stations and networks. Almost all stations and networks get their income from the sale of time for commercial messages.

Difficulties with commercials come from three sources: (1) When stations or networks oversell their inventory and too many commercials begin to compete with program time; (2) when advertisers produce messages that are deceptive or fraudulent; and (3) when the audience fails to understand that the commercial message provides only limited information, which is intended to persuade the viewers to buy.

The first problem is held in check by the economic forces of the media marketplace. Every reduction in program time involves the risk of the viewer switching channels. A reduction in the number of viewers lowers the efficiency of the medium as an advertising tool, thereby incurring a loss of income for stations and networks.

The marketplace is not as responsive to the second problem. Consequently, we have the Federal Trade Commission whose mandate is to police advertising practices. We also have several trade organizations that provide self-regulation. Commercials as persuasive messages are inherently susceptible to deceptive practices. The advertiser must make a constant effort to guard against slipping over the edge from reasonable aggrandizement to culpable fraud. They are not always successful.

We as teachers, parents, and viewers are responsible for the solution of the third problem. The commercial is a limited (albeit important) information source from a particular point of view. It is intended to sell the viewer; it is susceptible to deceptive practices; it is not required to tell "the whole story"; it will emphasize the good and not report the bad; it is not responsible to the consumer but to the seller; it is often attractive but subtle and deals in compelling motivations; and as an information source it has little competition. These facts form a primer for the competent viewer and consumer.

POLITICAL COMMERCIALS

Political advertising is an integral part of the American political system. Advertising in broadcasting is governed by some special rules established by the Communications Act and enforced by the FCC. In effect, no station has to sell advertising time to any candidate. However, if it sells time, it must do so at the lowest applicable rate and must make "equal time" available to all candidates for that same office. Last, the broadcaster has essentially no control over the content of the political commercial.

Political advertising on television has been touted to be enormously powerful. Books such as *The Selling of The President* have suggested that presidential candidates can be merchandized like toothpaste and detergent. Scientific research, however, has indicated that, election after election, interpersonal discussion and alliances are far more important in the decisions to vote and for whom to vote. In a series of studies on the last presidential race, findings show that most persons had decided on their candidate at or before the time of the conventions — months before the official campaign began. At present, the best interpretation of the effect of a campaign is twofold: (1) It establishes the agenda for discussion by identifying the candidates and the issues. The discussion itself and the decision will occur in interpersonal networks. (2) It provides a maintenance program for the decision once it is made. People who have chosen a candidate tend to avoid the advertisements of opposing candidates and to focus in on those of the candidate of their choice. Those latter advertisements provide ammunition in case an individual is drawn into discussion with a supporter of another candidate.

The five step analysis form used for product commercials can be readily adopted for analyzing political commercials. In addition, special attention should be paid to the techniques of image development used. The image of the candidate — strong, competent, understanding, whatever — is considered by campaign managers and social scientists alike as more important than the issues themselves. In many ways the notion makes sense. The specific issues of November will soon disappear over the four year term of a president. What remains important is how this person will react to stress, what kind of decision maker will evolve, and so on. Once again, the key to remember is that each element in a paid political advertisement has been planned for some persuasive purpose. Interviews are not spontaneous. Town meetings are very well staged with all members of the audience hand-picked. Even news events are controlled and staged as far as possible.

OTHER COMMERCIAL MESSAGES

There remains a potpourri of persuasive messages that appear on television. Two of the most common are the promotional announcements (promos) used by stations and networks to "sell" their own programs and the public service announcements (PSAs), which originate from governmental and other social agencies. Commercial stations almost exclusively promote their own product for obvious reasons. Occasionally a commercial station will sell time to promote a Public Television (PBS) program, but you're not going to find out about ABC programs from CBS promos.

Public Service Announcements appear as part of the station's responsibility for community service. PSAs usually occur at odd hours or when the time has not been sold commercially. The donation of a prime-time slot for a PSA is very expensive, but there is FCC pressure for it to occur on occasion. Despite some longings for it to be otherwise, the content of a PSA is not inherently truthful. Such announcements always represent some power group's point of view. The Agricultural Department, in its nutrition spots, advocates the use of food products for which there is a surplus for which it has to pay. The American Dental Association and similar professional groups have both political and professional positions, which if not espoused, at least, are not violated in their messages. For example, a dental spot about toothbrushes might include a closing comment to "see your dentist twice a year," a practice some medical researchers have argued against.

PSAs, then, are particularly difficult to analyze because they make use of specialized and often technical information not readily available to the audience. Some skepticism is warranted (remember the swine flu vaccination program), but on the other hand, they do serve the valuable purpose of transmitting useful information. The responsible consumer of information needs to maintain an openness to new material and at the same time be willing to reflect on potential sources of error and the costs involved.

Planning for Instruction

The chapter that follows will provide specific objectives and classroom activities regarding the use of television commercials to teach basic language and social studies concepts and skills. The information that has been presented here will provide the teacher with a rich background for integrating TV related activities into the regular program of instruction. It is recommended that you do not attempt to teach this information for its own sake, rather that you use it as you develop learning activities that relate closely to the daily experiences children have with television commercials.

Chapter 3

INSTRUCTIONAL OBJECTIVES
AND ACTIVITIES FOR TELEVISION
COMMERCIAL MESSAGES

CORE NOTIONS

MATERIAL in this area is directed by three fundamental concepts. (1) The television commercial is a prime source of product and merchandising information, but it is inherently biased by the intent to sell. That is, a commercial is judged successful when it persuades people to buy. It is not successful if it does no more than inform people. (2) Tests of utility can be applied to commercial information to guide the decision-making process. (3) People select products for certain purposes, although the purpose may not be readily apparent. Management of the selection process requires that we understand these purposes. Commercial persuasion attempts to manipulate the purposes that we have for selecting a product or service.

INQUIRY QUESTIONS FOR STUDENTS

- What things do I buy or have others buy for me?
- What things do I want but do not have?
- What good would the things I want do for me?
- Has some thing I wanted ever disappointed me after I obtained it?
- Why was I disappointed?
- How did I deal with that disappointment? What did I decide about the product or the source of my expectations?
- What is an advertiser?
- What are advertisements? Where do they appear? What is a commercial?
- What is a product? What is a brand name?
- What are an advertiser's responsibilities when telling us about

these products?

- How do advertisements help me learn about the things I want?
- How does TV tell me about things?
- Why does TV make toys look so exciting? Why are children shown having fun eating cereal?
- What do TV commercials leave out when they talk about their products?
- What is a supermarket?
- How does a supermarket or other display store work to sell products?
- How do shelf positioning, product grouping, store displays or promotions influence buying?
- What role does packaging play in our buying decisions?
- How can we test the information from commercials and other advertising sources?
- How can we test product performance?
- What would happen to television if we removed all commercials?
- What would change if we banned all advertising?

OBJECTIVES TO GUIDE SKILL BUILDING

The student will be able to demonstrate the following skills.

- Explain how a television commercial differs from an entertainment program.
- Identify the main purpose of a commercial as one of selling something.
- Demonstrate an understanding of the fact that people use television commercials to make decisions to buy products and services.
- Identify explicit and implicit promises that may be contained in audio and visual content of a television commercial.
- Identify appropriate means to evaluate the performance of a product and to determine the validity of the advertised promises.
- Differentiate among verbal, nonverbal, and visual content of a television commercial and to explain the intended effects of each in a specific commercial.
- Differentiate between the "intended effect" and the "actual effect" of a particular television commercial.
- Provide examples of TV commercials that respond to some indi-

vidual needs.

- Describe means by which a particular product claim can be evaluated to determine the worth of it.
- Recognize specific persuasive techniques that appear in selected commercials.
- Identify different types of commercial messages in terms of their purposes, e.g. selling products and services, good will, image building, public service, promotions of programs.
- Comprehend selected vocabulary that is commonly used in the study of television commercials, e.g. marketplace, identification, association, slice of life, product qualities, product evaluation, selling techniques.
- Describe ideal target audiences for specific commercials.
- Participate in the various aspects of creating and shooting a commercial.
- Identify the motivating purposes behind product purchases.
- Test product performance against the motivating purposes for buying.
- Demonstrate an ability to explain production decisions by participation in the preparation of a commercial.
- Explain the place of television commercials in our current mercantile system and in the competitive, free enterprise economy of the United States.

ACTIVITIES

In addition to these activities, the teacher should refer to the five steps for the evaluation of commercial messages and the discussions of the types of commercials presented in the previous chapter. The section at the end of this chapter has the necessary textual materials for a self-contained commercial analysis exercise.

DEVELOPING THE CONCEPT OF PERSUASION AND PERSUASIVE TECHNIQUES. This exercise is designed to provide the students with an insight into the differences between persuasion and information. Pose two problems for oral or written presentation: In the first, the task is to *inform* another about a decision that has been made about where the two of them are going to spend the afternoon. In the second, the task is to *persuade* the other to come along to the same place. Have the rest of the class observe the differences in language and style of delivery, particularly if the second child resists the persuasive attempts.

Once the commercial identification exercises that follow have been accomplished, the teacher may want to return to this difference by showing video-taped news stories in comparison with "pitchman" (single person exhorting a purchase) commercials.

COMMERCIAL IDENTIFICATION. Prepare the students for a viewing period by discussing these questions: What is a program? What is a commercial? How can we tell when a commercial message is presented on TV? How is the commercial different from the entertainment program? How is it the same? Preteach some basic vocabulary such as product, brand name, announcer, viewer, buyer. Provide a five to ten minute viewing segment (off-air or taped). Write the questions on the chalkboard and ask the students to consider each question as they view. Discuss the questions again, helping the students to answer them with the specific information from the segment viewed.

IDENTIFYING THE INTENT TO SELL. Have the students list some products they buy or others buy for them and products they have tried but did not like. Select a few products from each list and secure a videotape copy or an audio recording of the sound track or a few notes about commercials for those products. Help the students establish what was said by the commercial. Encourage them to explore why that information was presented. Then have them establish what else they would say about the products they use and like and about the products they do not like if they were talking to a good friend.

IDENTIFYING PERSUASIVE TECHNIQUES. Collect commercials that make use of the product quality claims and identification techniques. Have children view the commercials and identify the persuasive technique used in each.

ANALYSIS OF COMMERCIALS – TYPES AND DEVICES. Develop a videotape that has approximately seven separate commercials on it. The commercials should be representative of common types for products, services, and image building. Begin discussion about basic commercial goals. The children will have a variety of ideas but usually will center those ideas on commercials trying to sell something. Suggest that commercials try to do things other than just sell a product or service. A simplified category system can be developed through this discussion. Application of this category system can then be made to the commercials that are taped for class use.

If you prefer to move inductively, show the videotape, then work through a process of similarities and differences to arrive at the different goals of the messages.

To help the students identify effective visual devices, play the videotape (which they have now seen several times) with the screen dark (brightness turned down) and ask the children to identify the visual images that appear in their memory. Discuss why these images were memorable — what made them work. Then play only one commercial with the screen dark and ask the children to be ready to talk about the value of the visuals in transmitting that message. They might consider these questions: Would the commercial be just as effective without the visuals? What did the visuals "say" that was not said in the sound track? What visuals could be substituted for the ones used? Encourage the children to express their perceptions and to notice that not everyone is affected the same way.

Play the videotape again but with the sound off. Ask the children to decide what was lost from the commercial messages with no audio. Then play one commercial with the sound off and lead the discussion regarding the importance of both audio and visual effects in a television commercial.

In the analysis of effects, direct the students to consider the difference between the effects intended by the commercial producers and the actual feelings they had as viewers. In most cases the students will report that the commercial did not "work." Help them to determine the circumstances under which the commercial would work. For example, a soap commercial might never seem effective until one has to select a brand from a shelf full of soap in a supermarket.

The effect of this exercise can be heightened by judicious selection of the exemplar commercials. In the reduced sense modality presentations, commercials which are highly visually or aurally dependent can be compared with those where that sense modality plays a very secondary role. As noted before, description is very much vocabulary bound. Preteaching descriptive words, or working from a descriptive glossary, will greatly increase the effective expression of the students.

ANALYSIS OF COMMERCIALS — PROMISES, PROMISES. Beginning with advertisements from magazines or newspapers, aid the students to identify the explicit and implicit promises contained with the messages. Many newspaper and magazine ads are part of a multi-media campaign. The print advertisements repeat the same basic theme as the television commercial for the product. If possible, then, identify advertisements that appear in print and in television and secure copies in both media. Once the students have gained some experience in identifying promises within print messages, secure a videotape of a selection of commercials. Explain to the students that this viewing will help them to recognize actual promises and implied or thinly disguised promises and that they will have the chance to think about the way that different commercials affect them. Provide an example of an implied promise and of an explicit or direct promise. Ask them to give other examples of each. Keep in mind that some children may have difficulty in expressing the implied promise, although they may be able to act upon them. Also, remember that an effective implied promise is easily perceived by many persons as a direct promise.

ANALYSIS OF PRODUCTS — PURPOSE AND PERFORMANCE. Analysis of the performance of any product must begin with the purpose for which it was purchased. It does one little good to buy an excellent screwdriver to drive a nail. The purpose and the product simply do not mesh. On the other hand, cheap toys with little life expectancy may be just the thing to ensure that each child at a party gets a prize when the party giver's budget is limited. The teacher can begin this exercise by having the students list the products they buy or have others buy for them. Consider the purposes that each of these products can have. Determine which purposes the products can well serve, which ones the products cannot. Tie these purposes in with the promises that are offered in advertisements for the products. How can a cola drink promise good times or an automobile promise status? Help the students identify products and purposes that are inappropriately matched in commercial messages.

PRODUCTION OF COMMERCIALS IN CLASS. Preplanning is the key to a successful commercial. The planning begins with the product to be sold and the identification of the qualities that lend themselves to selling. Any product will work, but there appears to be more educational merit in using a product for which there is no commercial form to imitate. The authors tend to select objects like rocks, earth, wood, an abstract form which will force the students to an analysis of selling qualities. Once the product and its qualities have been determined, the decisions as to target audience, persuasive techniques, textual approach, sound effects, visuals, and other production values must be made.

Organize the children into five member commercial preparation teams. Each team should independently decide upon the product to be sold (or the image to be built or the good feeling to be sought) and should deal with all other decisions. You may want to require that each member of the team write a script for the commercial. It takes about 75 words for a 30 second commercial. The team can then decide which of the five scripts it wants to produce. Responsibilities for preparing the visuals, producing sound effects, camera work, and acting should be shared by the team members. The experience, of course, is the aim.

The students should rehearse their commercials until they are sufficiently prepared that they can meet the goals of their script. Tape a dress rehearsal and discuss with them ways in which they can improve for the final take. Further advice on in-school productions is contained in Chapter 8.

Class viewing of the final take of the pupil-made commercials should be done one or two days later to provide time for pupil reflection and team discussion regarding their work. Motivation will be high in the viewing sessions. This condition provides an excellent opportunity to return to what was learned in the analysis of commercial techniques and promises. Prior to viewing, help the students devise a simple checklist for evaluating each commercial.

After an initial screening, go through the same procedures as in the analysis of devices — play the commercials without video and without audio. Have the students identify successful and unsuccessful techniques.

Have the students jot down the implied and direct promises. Discuss whether the viewers list agrees with the production team's intent. Help the students to understand that it is to be expected that there will be a variety of responses because the "effect" depends upon the individual viewer perceptions.

A great deal of student interest and motivation can be generated for the study of commercials by involving the students immediately in making their own commercials. The initial experience with commercials will reveal many areas of information and skill that go into producing commercials for television and a purpose for further study will be established. Obviously, an alternative approach is to read and discuss all aspects of commercials before involving the students in making commercials. It is clear the teacher should proceed in a manner that makes most sense individually.

In making a commercial at upper grade levels, organize the students in five member advertising agency teams as with younger pupils. At this level, students can experience the process of identifying a client and tailoring a commercial message to that client's needs for a product or service. Enlist the aid of other teachers or administrative personnel who have a need for publicity. Perhaps a coach would like a commercial of an athletic meet or the librarian would like to encourage the reading of books and so on. Once you have identified potential clients for the students, have them negotiate the terms of a simple contract, specifying the rights and duties of each party.

When the client and the product or service have been identified, the team should proceed through production as described earlier. We might note that it is particularly useful to have the entire class analyze each commercial and discuss the differences between intent and actual effect.

One of the major payoffs for the production team is that the commercial actually gets used for its intended purpose — publicity. Parent meetings, teacher meetings, athletic group meets, special events, can all provide audiences for these works.

RATINGS AND TARGET AUDIENCES. Divide the class into advertiser teams. Assign to each team a product commonly advertised on television. Instruct the teams to determine the target audience for the product in relation to a particular selling approach (cars, for example can be sold to various target audiences depending on the approach). Obtain a copy of a program ratings book from your local television station. Better, invite the sales manager to meet with the class, telling him/her of the exercise in progress. Ask the sales manager to provide a two or three program sample buy for each team's target audience. Should the sales manager not be available (though they usually are) select two or three programs from the ratings book that show high circulation for that target audience. Discuss with the students why that program appeals to that audience and why an advertiser interested in reaching an audience of that type would buy time during the program for a commercial.

ANALYTICAL EXERCISES. Have the students complete an outside viewing assignment. Ask the students to take notes on at least five commercials that they see overnight or on the weekend. Have them record the selling technique that was used and indicate the conditions under which they thought each would be effective. This simple question outline can be used: What was the product or service in the commercial? What was the target audience? What selling technique was used? Under what conditions do you think it would work?

SUPERMARKET FIELD TRIP. After your class has completed the commercial analysis and production exercises, arrange with the manager of the local supermarket for a field trip visit. Many television commercial messages are designed to be effective at the point of purchase, in the store, when the buying decision must be made. Divide the class into teams and assign to each team the selection of some household item for which there are a variety of brands available. Have each team arrive at a decision as to which brand to buy. Have them record the brands available and the information the group had about each. Should sufficient time be available this is an excellent time to point out techniques of comparison shopping, how to read product labels, and unit pricing.

In classroom discussion, consider the decisions of each purchase team. Have them report on the brands available, the information available to the team, the processes by which the decision was made, and of course, the final decision. Help them to identify any points where television or other media advertising may have influenced their decisions.

THE ECONOMIC ROLE OF COMMERCIALS. Discuss with the class some background questions, such as, why do we have to put up with commercials that interrupt our TV viewing? Does anyone protect us from advertising that is not telling the truth? What would happen to all the brands of toothpaste if we got rid of commercial advertising?

It is not of critical importance that the students master all of the special terms that appear in the reading. The vocabulary will help them, however, to think about and talk about the work of the television and advertising industries. Review with the students the following terms: commercials, advertisements, products, brand name, services, image building, prime time, target audiences. Introduce the terms circulation, market, advertising agency, time slot, revenue, expenses, and profit.

The economics of the ratings process will deserve considerable discussion. It would be good to bring in the local station manager or sales manager to talk about ratings, circulation, and time sales, as these affect directly what we see on television. A class meeting with the manager would be a profitable culmination of this exercise.

Related Activities

1. Prepare a worksheet children can use to categorize commercials according to the selling technique used.
2. Prepare a bulletin board to illustrate the function commercials play in the television industry.
3. Write a commercial using the "slice of life" format. The competence format.
4. Develop a step-by-step procedure that will guide children to write their own commercials for a mutually determined product.
5. Prepare a list of as many positioning labels as possible.
6. Develop a supermarket activity that will help the children pinpoint similarities and differences in packaging. Are several products intended for the same purpose similarly packaged? What are those products? What is it about a certain package that catches your eye?
7. List the characteristics children can use to identify Public Service Announcements.
8. Organize a survey to be conducted by the students. Include various product categories (cleaning aids, beauty products, breakfast foods, etc.). Examples of questions to be included in the survey are: What *dishwashing soap* do you use? How long have you been using it? Why did you first try that brand? Why do you use it?
9. Develop a simulation game that focuses on television commercials. In the game, honesty and accuracy will be rewarded by in-

creased buying of the product. Dishonesty will be punished by restrictions being placed on availability of advertising time or removal of the product from the market.

10. Prepare, for presentation in your class, a five minute address that you would give to a parent group in which you inform them of the ways in which the study of television commercials will build important basic language and social studies skills.

11. Pay special attention to the commercial announcements during a one hour program segment. Prepare a worksheet to help pupils identify to what age group the commercial was directed; to what sex the commercial was directed; the primary outcome resulting from the use of the product; the secondary outcome resulting from the use of the product; and the reality or fictionality of the claims made by the commercial.

Chapter 4

USING ENTERTAINMENT PROGRAMS
TO EXTEND BASIC SKILLS

THE entertainment content of any medium has always been subjected to close scrutiny and generous criticism by persons and organizations who fear that the youth of the nation may be morally damaged by "undesirable" books, magazines, movies, and dramatic productions. At various times in many communities in the United States, novels like *Catcher in the Rye, Slaughterhouse Five, Forever Amber,* and *Lady Chatterly's Lover* have been removed from the shelves of school and public libraries. Magazines such as *Hustler* and *Penthouse* have encountered difficulty with "decency boards" in cities large and small, and some city police departments have taken action to keep R and X rated movies out of their theatres.

Television entertainment has come under the same sort of scrutiny, and there have been efforts to control what is shown. Due to the nationwide audience of the major networks, and the considerable income a local station may receive from showing a controversial prime time show, the success of efforts to control is indeed small.

Many parents and child advocates have expressed concern that violent television programs would encourage violent behavior by the young viewers, that sexual content in TV would weaken the morals of the young, and that the plots of television would provide the young viewers with a warped concept of the real world. In Gerbner's view, there is good reason to be concerned about TV programs that tell stories about *how things work* in real life.

The entertainment programs of television do tell many stories about *how things work* in real life; in fact, most of their stories are of this sort. Stories of value and choices in life are frequently woven into the plots of many entertainment programs. One need only recall the furor caused by a planned abortion on the *Maude Show,* the racist humor of *Archie Bunker,* and the sexual entanglements on *Soap* to recognize that many adult Americans consider such shows to be

59

telling about how things work.

What responsibility does the school have to prepare young people to critically view and evaluate the entertainment program of television? It seems reasonable to expect that the school should help its students to build skills and concepts for the critical use of television just as children are prepared to be critical and thoughtful readers of printed material.

Four questions concerning the young viewers of entertainment programs will provide direction to the development of our instruction here.

1. What reality is perceived by the child as he views fictional comedy or action drama (*Bugs Bunny* and *Chips*)?
2. Do children learn social behavior and roles from the programs they watch?
3. How does the child deal with values projected in the TV programs they watch?
4. Can the child critically analyze a TV program?

These questions are just as appropriately asked regarding the child's use of printed material. The development of the skills of critical analysis of televised program content should be seen as improving the communication skills that are basic to the effective use of any medium. All four of these questions hold implications for the school's efforts to develop the child's abilities to appreciate literary and dramatic qualities of both televised and print materials. The child's familiarity with the formats, plots, and characters of television entertainment programs provides a most appropriate beginning point for the development of analysis and appreciation of the content of any medium.

Perceived Reality

"Is that real?" "Did that really happen?" "How did they do that?" Such questions are often fielded by parents and older children as they watch with the young viewer. Television drama and comedy have moved sharply away from the obvious or contrived situations common ten years ago. The urban crime drama is often a chilling reminder of what is read as news or seen on the streets. Situation comedies have adopted families much like our own or our neighbor's. It is not surprising that a young viewer might become confused as to whether or not an event is real.

The problem is further compounded by the fact that television substantially reshapes even those real events it presents. A news story compresses a fire into a thirty-second presentation focusing on the visually exciting and colorful aspects. Documentaries are highly edited, presenting unified statements from unorganized, dissimilar events. The perspective of camera and microphone is unique to the medium and is not fundamental to the methods by which we know that the rain is really wet or the sun really hot. Television then is an event of and by itself. It is not an imitation of anything.

The problem of reality occurs when one attempts to transfer information from one context (television) to another (our interaction with others). For example, research has shown that people who have limited contacts outside the home and who are also high consumers of television drama tend to perceive the outside world as more dangerous and crime ridden than those who have many contacts outside the home. Such individuals can be considered as using the television information to make decisions about real life events.

Assume we are watching an urban crime drama such as *Starsky and Hutch*. One reality question might be: Do the characterizations presented represent a good approximation of how police operate? If not, what are the differences between the televised view and the view we might get by accompanying a local police officer? Children have little difficulty in making judgments about the televised view and the view provided by their own experience. When conflict exists they typically choose their own experience. Problems do arise when the child has no experience against which to compare television "information."

There are two major classroom approaches we can use to deal with the problems of perceived reality: (1) we can provide experiences that can be used to confirm or refute televised information; (2) we can instruct students in the characteristics of the information presented.

The first approach is an application of the notion of directed experience, with which we are all familiar. One comment might be useful: It is surprising to us, at least, how little many children know of the world of work. Most children are unable to provide even a close approximation of the work activities of their parents. Television, on the other hand, often shows selected, idealized views of the world of work. Direct experiences in this area could be particularly profitable.

The second area requires us to analyze the factors that shape the information presented by television. We can categorize these factors into ten separate elements as we perceive them within the context of the entertainment program: (1) the compression and extension of visual and aural space; (2) the editorial perspective of camera and microphone; (3) the compression and extension of time; (4) the juxtaposition of images and events; (5) the traditional dependence on the aural track for presentation of plot progressing information; (6) the control of information by author and director in terms of amount and timing; (7) the dramatic intent of the information; (8) the willing suspension of disbelief by the audience; (9) the effect of commercial interruption; and (10) the program format. Each of these factors controls and/or modifies the information we receive. The action of each is described below.

Compression and Extension of Visual and Aural Space

Camera lenses and microphones do not maintain the distances our eyes see and our ears hear. Wide angle lenses that present the covering or establishing shot enlarge the distances between objects, making a space appear much larger than it is. Rooms become more spacious; vistas more grand. Narrow-angle or telephoto lenses shorten the distances between objects, moving people and things closer together. Action is more intense, quicker (action toys are shown in close-up for that reason). Microphones enlarge a voice and give it a presence that can be maintained over distance. Normally, a voice loses that presence as distance increases.

The Editorial Perspective of Camera and Microphone

An important part of perspective is the editing function. What is not shown or heard is often more important to the full understanding of a bit of information than what is. A few bricks in close-up could be the Great Wall of China; a baseball park could be full if the empty seats are not shown. The viewer is typically denied the whole picture and, consequently must fill in the context in which the visual information is presented. Aural information is similarly manipulated. Excitement can be generated by turning up the crowd noise; laughter can be inserted after a "joke."

The Compression and Extension of Time

Television usually compresses time, editing out most of the steps from A to B. Travelogues tour a country in an hour, removing the grind of driving from place to place. Time compression makes many activities seem much simpler than they actually are. Time can also be extended. A director may film an action from several vantage points and edit the shots together to show the same action again and again but from differing viewpoints. The instant replay extends time. The fan in the stadium becomes well aware of the advantages of the replay when someone blocks his view of the winning play.

The Juxtaposition of Images and Events

We interpret what we see and hear by what we have seen and heard. The process of editing — putting visual and aural information together — controls the display of information and establishes the meaning we will attach to each element. Eisenstein, pioneer film theorist, showed that viewers would impute all levels of pathos to a passive facial expression when the preceeding context suggested it. Events can also be arranged in time through editing, and because order can be manipulated, one event may be seen as pressaging another when it should not.

Dependence on Aural Track for Presentation of Plot Information

In most television programs, visual information is subordinate to aural information in regards to advancing the plot or developing characterization. The visual track is typically used for excitement, color, and impact. The visual scene usually lacks continuity but is, rather, a collection of effects bound together by expository dialogue. In essence, the television program manipulates the visual presentation at will while maintaining the dramatic form in sound. One can demonstrate this effect by watching others view. A common viewing process for children finds them doing homework while "watching" television. Actually they are listening and attend to the screen only when the aural track cues them that a change has occurred or some visually important event is about to be presented.

Control of Information by Author and Director

In any literary presentation we know only what the author cares to tell us and only when it is presented. We have no independent source of information against which to verify. Personalities are formed by what characters are permitted to do. Whereas in our everyday concourse we can make good predictions about those we know, the television character is free to perform in any manner. The addition of auralization and visualization of events may lead one to perceive an independent source of information. Of course what the person sees and hears has been selected for him by the director and the editor. The viewer will never see what they do not want her to see. We should not input sinister motives; this control is the foundation of artistic creation. All that is necessary is for the viewer to realize that each program is an artistic rendering.

Simply stated, the creative team's responsibility is to the progression of the plot; it is not to the veracity of what is presented. No one would require Shakespeare to present an actual approximation of a midsummer's night dream. It was his creative license to present a fantasy. Realism is only necessary if it is required to advance the plot. Understanding the dramatic intent is clearly a fundamental element in the evaluation of what is presented.

Willing Suspension of Disbelief

It is the tradition of theatre that when we participate in drama we will enter the context of the play — the mind. We must be willing to grant the deceits, large and small, that are necessary for thematic development. The question we began with ("Is it real?") is, of course, inappropriate to the dramatic form. Children need assurance that all dramatic entertainment makes use of fantasy and fiction.

Effects of Commercial Interruption

Commercial interruptions affect content and viewers. The content of a program must take into account the regular break necessary for the commercial. Each half-hour is commonly divided into thirds, with each segment having separate responsibilities while being dependent on the whole. The viewer comes to expect these breaks, but at times can find them quite disorienting, particularly if well immersed in the presentation.

Program Format

In addition to the limitation determined by the need for commercial interruptions, the format of the program itself imposes requirements on the development of plot and story line. In a series, the continuing characters will, of course, survive. In a half-hour program, the plot resolution will be reached at somewhere close to twenty-six minutes and thirty seconds. The nature of programs becomes highly predictable, so much so that viewers show less than 3 percent error in prediciting when a program will start, be interrupted, start again, and conclude. Both the commercial interruptions and the program formats make the artifice of the presentation visible and, thus, according to dramatic theory, lessen the dramatic impact of the program. The familiarity of the format gives the viewer a comfortable environment and reduces the amount of effort necessary to track the developing plot, much the same as formula novels. Programs that violate these expectations can actually be met with some hostility.

"Is that real?" "Well, it's really television." "How come that man can fly, and I can't?" "Because he's a person on television and you're a person in real life." Helping children distinguish among, and evaluate, different information sources has always been a key educational objective.

Social Learning

Research has indicated that children who have reduced access to other information sources will make use of television to fill in those information blanks. Children, as they become more involved in the process of social assimilation, may be particularly sensitive to the presentation of social situations on entertainment programs.

Our observational studies provide a good example. These studies involved working with families as they watch television. In one family with a history of one job transfer after another, the twelve year old daughter's favorite programs were those which had main characters of that age. The daughter noted that she liked those programs because they helped her learn what to do in different situations. While the young woman was in no way handicapped socially, her friendships tended to be less secure and, consequently, less useful for social learning. The television program became her laboratory, providing and testing ideas.

Even without special circumstances, younger children are continually striving for information about the world of older children that they are about to enter. A daughter of one of the authors was explaining what it meant to "park." She said, "First you turn the radio on loud. Then, you find someplace dark and open the windows. Then, you get close together and kiss, I guess." When asked how she knew all this, she replied, "Oh, I learned it all on *Happy Days.*" This little story exemplifies the preconditions for social learning: First, there has to be an interest or need on the part of the child. Second the program content has to be appropriate to the child's information requirements and to the child's ability to understand. Third, if the information is going to be useful, the author must have creatively captured the essence of the event or interaction.

It is this latter point that leads us to the critical skill area. When we evaluate a dramatic scene we do so on the basis of our experience or from an extension of our experience. A successful scene "fits" and extends what we know about life. The child tends to be less critical, less analytical, because he operates from a more limited experiential base. Surely, one solution is to share our experience with the child. One of the easiest ways to do this is to work through short scenes taken from entertainment programs providing a synopsis of the characters, situation, and plot development.

Value Formation

While there are many definitions, let us consider a value as something that consistently directs behavior and provides a criterion by which the "worth" of an action may be established. One's values are shown by what a person does. The consistent actions of television characters also exhibit the values that have been created in the characterization. The "worth" of these consistent actions can be transferred to the viewer. If a character consistently uses violence to solve problems, she obviously attaches substantive worth to the solution. We know that children can and will learn the behaviors that are presented. Whether they will produce those behaviors depends on whether they consider them valuable to their own ends.

Information and value sources are most effective where there is a vacuum. If the child has an effective value structure of his own, we would expect other value sources to have little influence. On the other hand, where there is uncertainty, value conflict, or the absence of values, the preconditions for influence are established. The effect of television can be described with the following analogy to light: Consider the influence of television to be like a flashlight. Consider the influence of parents, peers, the societal institutions of school, church, etc. to be like the sun. Take a flashlight out on a bright, sunny day and it is difficult to tell it is on. For the child in shadow, cut off from those dominating influences, the flashlight can become a beacon.

Children's values develop in such a way that they may not be able to define them in words. More often than not, something just feels wrong. If those feelings conflict with what they see on television, the child may become unsure of her standards. Our contribution can be to identify the values the continuing characters represent and to indicate that other values may lead to other solutions. The knowledge that others may not feel good about some consistent way a TV problem is solved can be very reassuring to a child who is unfamiliar with a value conflict that involves a favorite character.

One classroom approach would be to work out descriptions, with the children, of their favorite TV characters. These descriptions would provide the qualities and the value of those qualities that the child assigns to each character (from our experience children will positively value those characters who represent the values expressed at home; when there are substantial differences, it can represent a temporary or long-standing conflict area for the child). Once the descriptions have been developed, further explorations of values can be accomplished through the ambiguous situation technique. This method makes use of common problem situations — "you just found a dollar bill; what do you do with it?" — and asks the child to provide solutions. The solutions might include what the child would do, what various TV characters would do, what the right thing would be, and so on.

Fifth and sixth grade children will certainly be ready to participate in a process of value analysis. This process embodies three steps: value identification, value clarification, and value judgment. Value identification is the development of a definition couched in behavioral terms. Values are best defined in behavioral terms because the notion of a value is only a conceptual aid to help us to deal with consistencies of behavior we observe in others. The value of honesty, for example, as with any value, is best explained through a series of anecdotes of the behaviors of honest people. Value identification helps the child develop behavioral terms for what.it means to be truthful, peace-loving, aggressive, cynical, etc. Value identification can, of course, begin by looking for behavior consistencies. Children's television characters are usually developed with an observable degree of rigidity in value expression. They are consequently somewhat less lifelike, but good sources of examples for values.

Value clarification involves the application of the value to differing situations. Value clarification explores the consequences of holding a value. What solutions to the dollar bill questions would come from an honest person, a miserly one? Value clarification also involves discussion of value conflict. An individual is often faced with situations where different values suggest different courses of action. Value clarification indicates these points of conflict and helps the child establish the scope or the limits of a value.

The last step is value judgment, which is the comparison of the behavioral consequences of a particular value with the consequences of those values held personally, held by the family, or promoted by social institutions, and the analysis of the worth of each. The process of value judgment is an important intervention between the media presentation and the child. Instruction in value judgment provides the child with techniques of careful examination of the extended consequences of behaving in certain ways.

The primary analytical technique is that of projection. One need only to establish a situation and then to project characters with different values into that situation and consider the behavioral results. One of those characters should be the individual. The plot of the television entertainment program can provide several ready-made situations.

There is little question that more than a little care must be taken when dealing in the area of values. The teacher must work to preserve a positive, nonpejorative atmosphere. There are, of course, many approaches to the same problem. To suggest that one is better than another runs some risk. A neutral exploration of the consequences of a given solution is generally more satisfactory.

The Child as Critic

The preceding three sections have laid a sound foundation for the child to function as a critic. What remains is to shift the focus from the viewer back to the program. Critical analysis is most useful when it can be shared, when we have a common set of inspection points so that we may compare our results with others. The following is one such set. First, a few definitions are needed to get us off to a good start.

Plot — The developing or unfolding interaction among story-line, motivating elements, and characterization.

Story line — A serial description of events and their temporal and causal connections.

Motivating elements — Initial and subsequent conditions that provide explanation for action.

Characters — Individuals about whom the audience has gained some knowledge. They may or may not put in an appearance.

Characterization — What we know about the character that gives the individual substance and establishes expectations of future behavior.

Theme — The message, moral, or overall meaning of the plot; the underlying assumptions, which dictate the resolution of the plot.

Program format — The external constraints on the dramatic form — time frame of the program, commercial interruptions, standards and practices, the program as part of a series, contractual agreements, and so on.

Production values — The aural and visual elements and processes by which the plot is presented; these would include camera work, music, sound effects, settings, lighting, etc.

Using these basic notions we can develop a number of questions to direct our analysis of a program. A few exemplars under each major heading follow:

STORY LINE

- What is the synopsis of the story — what was the story about?
- Describe the setting in time and place.
- Is the story complete; conflicts resolved; fate of all delineated characters known? Or, are there unanswered questions?
- Does the story have a defined beginning and ending or is it a point of passage, an incident in the life of the characters?
- If it is a point of passage, are the initial conditions adequately presented and plausible?
- Is the story primarily a vehicle for physical action, description, character exposition, comedic elements?

CHARACTERS AND CHARACTERIZATION

- Identify the characters.
- Give a physical description of the characters.
- Describe the personality qualities of each delineated character.
- How are the characters developed in actions, speech, appearance, gesture, facial expression? What was memorable or notable about each?
- Is the characterization adequately developed so that the character's actions are understandable? Do you want to know more about the character? Are there elements of the characterization that simply draw attention to themselves?
- Is the characterization appropriate to the plot and theme(s)? That is, do the characterizations fit the generic requirements for realism, stereotype, or the requirements of the specific dramatic form — comedy, slapstick, surrealism, etc.?
- Are the characterizations reliable or do elements appear and disappear without reason?
- Do the characters change in personality or action? If so, is the change prepared for adequately and executed in a believable fashion?
- Does a characterization attain more importance than story line?
- Which character is most believable? With whom do you identify or sympathize the most?
- What segment(s) of society are most of the characters drawn

from? What level of education and income do most characters have? Does a single sex, race, or other distinguishing characteristic of the actors predominate?

- If a certain actor type predominates, are there exceptions to the rule? What happens to the characters played by these actors?

MOTIVATING ELEMENTS

- Describe the motivating elements derived from the characters and characterization, external forces, fate, nature, etc.
- Is each major action adequately motivated? Or, do actions appear that are unexplained?
- What motivates the main agent of the action? Does the agent encounter any resistance from another person, society, nature, or him/herself?
- Are new motives introduced? If so, is the introduction plausible or simply convenient?

PLOT AND THEME

- Identify the conflicts presented: man versus man; man versus self; man versus nature.
- Were the conflicts resolved or did the plot simply show another incident in the conflict?
- Did the presentation of the conflict aim at the exposition of some theme or message or was the conflict simply a vehicle for action effects?
- Were the conflict and resolution believable, well motivated? Were the conflicts trivial or important? Were the conflicts something you might be involved with in real life or were they artificially created for the sake of the show and the characters?
- Was the plot development predictable? Was the outcome ever in doubt? Do you have a strong hint from the beginning as to what the resolution would be?
- At what point in the show are the conflicts revealed? How are the conflicts revealed?
- Are there any subplots? Are these subplots necessary to develop the main conflict or are they cameo plots?
- What is the theme(s) of the plot? Is it explicitly stated or in the deep background? Is it controversial, for effect, trivial, etc.?
- How does the treatment of the theme compare with other treatments?

- Can you follow a line of development from beginning to middle to end in terms of plot and theme presentation?
- Does the plot build to a coherent climax or are there many subclimaxes or is the action simply dissipated?
- Does the denouement following the climax provide an adequate explanation for the resolution?
- Is there a balance between story line and characters or does one dominate?

PROGRAM FORMAT

- Does the show depend on the same cast of characters each week? If so, do they show development? Do the plots progress or do they become a collection of character routines?
- Does the time frame of the program affect plot development? Are commercial breaks provided for by breaks in the "action"? Does the climax come at the same time each week?
- Are the commercials a welcome break or an intrusion? Are they well placed?
- What audience does the program appeal to? How does the program fit into the "line up" for that day-part period?
- Is the program typical of programs of its class? Is it innovative or a copy?
- If part of a series, does the program repeat the same theme, plot structure, character development? Does the program have a predictable routine?

PRODUCTION VALUES

- Is the camera an integral part of plot and character development or is it simply a window to the dramatic world?
- Is sound used for a dramatic purpose, e.g. music or special sound effects?
- Are the settings appropriate to the plot? Are they believable? Are they well-used, under-used, over-used?
- Does the costuming support the characterization? Is it appropriate to the period and place?
- Is the pacing appropriate to the program and plot?
- Is the dialogue worth listening to? Is it appropriate to the program?
- Are there effects or techniques that are distracting (e.g. laugh tracks, lighting effects, etc.)?

VOCABULARY REQUIREMENTS

The ability to analyze appears to be closely tied to developmental state. As the child grows older powers of discernment increase rapidly. For many children, however, analytical problems occur not because they do not perceive elements and differences but because they lack the vocabulary to describe them. A good part of the instruction in criticism would be the development of adequate terminology.

Summary

Critical analysis is composed of two major parts. The first is a description of the work — what is there. The second is the assignment of value — its worth. We are perhaps most successful in valuation when we describe worth in relation to some purpose. What is it good for? Criticism in relationship to some goal that can be behaviorally expressed relieves us from the burden of determining *what ought* to be and allows us to deal with *what is*.

Chapter 5

INSTRUCTIONAL ACTIVITIES
FOR ENTERTAINMENT CONTENT

OBJECTIVES are useful in providing specific direction to any individual activity. They are particularly important in situations that make use of innovative material, such as television programming where the opportunities for distraction are plentiful. The objectives provided here have been used (with students from age 9 to 16 years) in pilot programs in public schools. They have been helpful in determining which programs to use for class instruction, and they offer an adequate reference for evaluating the extent to which the pupils have mastered concepts and skills.

The following list of objectives suggests a minimum statement of goals for this curriculum. As with all sets of objectives, the individual teachers will make final judgment as to those that are appropriate for various age levels. It is expected that objectives will be pursued at more than one age/grade level for purposes of skill maintenance and refinement.

Skill Objectives for Entertainment Content

- Recognize when the extension and compression of time and space are used for specific effects in TV content.
- Describe the intended effects of background sound and pictorial setting as it relates to mood and character development.
- Tell, in a brief statement, the story line of a TV entertainment program.
- Describe the plot of a TV program in terms of the interaction among story line, setting, characterization, and the motivating elements.
- Describe the kinds of characters needed to develop a given story line.
- Identify the major and minor characters in a program and explain the value of each character to the plot development.

- Identify and describe the major types of TV entertainment programs.
- Explain the difference between characters and actors in a dramatic presentation
- Identify and describe the conflicts and problems that are typically used in favorite programs.
- Describe the motivation of the major characters as it explains their actions in the plot.
- Identify the conflict in the program and explain its necessity to the plot.
- Identify the strongly held values of major characters as expressed in their actions and in the resolution of conflict and problems
- Discuss the effects that specific TV characters have on viewers in terms of a desire to be like the character, to like or dislike the character, to enjoy the character, and so forth.
- Make descriptive comments concerning the production values of the program — music, special effects, camera work.
- Explain the effect of continuing characters on plot development.
- Evaluate the information presented in entertainment programs in terms of its utility to different settings in real life.
- Recognize underlying themes in programs and program series.
- Classify the conflict or problem that is used in a specific program (man against nature, man against fate).

ACTIVITIES

These activities can provide useful approaches to the attainment of the learning objectives for entertainment content. In addition to these activities, Chapter 4 presented some approaches to social learning, value analysis, and aesthetic inquiry.

UNIQUE PERSPECTIVE OF CAMERA AND MICROPHONE. Introduce the notion of a camera and of a microphone. Relate it to the eyes and ears of the television set. Discuss with the class their thoughts about the ability of a camera and microphone to show and tell everything about an event, such as a football game or a rodeo. This will set the stage for experimentation with a view box (see workbook section for instructions) or paper tubes through which children can view objects from different distances. Instant camera photographs of objects at different distances and angles will show both the limitations and creative interpretations that can occur.

Set up the television camera. Rehearse a short scene of one person talking to four others. Two of them can show approval, the other two disapproval. Record the scene first showing only the approving audience, second the disapproving audience, and third both sets. Discuss with the class how the camera gives a different interpretation of the same scene. Be prepared to exploit the problems in "blocking" (setting the relative positions of) the camera and the actors. The scene will work best when shot over the shoulder of the speaker looking at the audience, but let the students experiment with a side to side relationship, which is more natural to eyesight.

Record the voices of the children at various distances and angles to show microphone limitations. Use this opportunity to have children produce background sound for specific effects, such as the sounds of surprise, anticipation, joy, a crowd of people, and so forth.

SOUND IMAGES. Play a record or a tape of music such as "Sleep Little Dogies" and have the children suggest a story and the action that would go with it. Some commercials have distinct musical themes or jingles. These can be recorded and the images they evoke discussed by the students.

With an audio cassette recorder, record common sounds such as traffic, water running, a door slamming, a car door. Develop a short matching test to be sure everyone participates. Use the sound effects as background to one of the stories in the reader.

Show a videotape segment or a short movie with the sound turned off to help the students comprehend the part that sound plays in developing the mood of a situation and in emphasizing the qualities of characters. Play a videotaped segment or movie with the brightness turned down or the projector lamp off to help the students understand how the story develops in sound and dialogue more than in pictures.

CONTROL OF TIME AND SPACE. Almost every television story compresses time and distance. Recording short segments will provide a library of examples. Have the students make estimates of the amount of time deleted or the missing parts of a process. The instant replay on most sports programs is a good example of the expansion of time.

Discuss with the children ways by which they can show that time has passed by dramatizing the passage of time from childhood to old age.

Exercises in Extracting Story Lines. Provide the children with three or four story lines from popular TV programs such as *The Waltons* or *Little House on the Prairie.* Discuss with the children just what a story line tells you. Select a short story that the class has recently read. Review it with them and help them extract the story line. Help them to limit their descriptions to a recitation of events and their interrelationships. The students might be able to write the story line of a program they saw the night before. Creative expression would have them write a story line that they would like to see on their favorite TV program. Story line elements (events) can be listed on the board and the students can use them to construct a story line by providing the connections between them. A discussion of the story lines that result will highlight the differences that can occur in the creative process.

Exercises in Recognizing Pictorial Setting. Have students select pictures from magazines to represent different pictorial settings listed on the board. Discuss how the elements in the picture develop the setting. Have the children test what could be left out of the scene without markedly changing the setting. Discuss what could be added to improve it.

Help the students identify the setting of their favorite programs. Show how story lines can move from setting to setting (*Star Wars* is now called a modern, medieval morality play).

Textual Analysis. A number of the objectives may be pursued through the use of materials and experiences that are a part of the on-going reading and language development programs. For example, an understanding of the term "story line" can be approached in the reading and discussion of short stories in reading class. A grasp of the relationship between character development and plot can be similarly advanced. It will be necessary to ensure transfer of these skills to televised materials through their application to content from that medium. The point is well made, however, that the basic concepts and skills may be reasonably initiated through the basic reading and language programs. There have been a number of well-developed programs of textual analysis. One approach would include the following. Select a short story that has been read by the entire class, preferably one of high interest. Have the students read the story again to answer these questions: Who were the people in the story? How did they behave? What problems did they face? How did they attempt to solve them? What characters could be left out without ruining the story? What events occurred? How were the events related? What solutions did the author provide? What other solutions might be given?

Discuss the responses of the students. On their first attempt it is most likely that students will not do well. Among other elements, the analysis requires a vocabulary the student may not have developed.

Prepare a simple dramatic script of the story with the students. Discuss how each character would speak and act, what the character would say. Have the students cast their classmates in the parts, explaining why they made their choices. Help the students develop characterizations for the various parts. Characterization through dramatization of a story enlarges the perception the reader first had. Investigate the different requirements of the script form versus the short story form.

Discuss the process of characterization. Do you become a character in the story and develop it according to your own insights? Or do you act in the way that you think the author wanted the character to be seen? Consider the differences in the judgments that a character in a play might make as compared with the ones the actor as a person might make. Discuss the meaning of actor and character to reinforce their separation. Is it possible to play the part of a character that you would not like to be in real life? As the students develop their characterizations, have them explain why they have their characters behave in certain ways in order to identify the elements that motivate the characters.

Make plans to record the dramatization. Help the students to block the actors' movements; work out a shot list for the camera. Rotate the students through the various parts and recording tasks. Compare the recordings and consider the differences.

ANALYSIS OF TELEVISED MATERIAL. Secure VTR play back equipment and a videotape of segments from four or five entertainment programs of different types. After each presentation discuss with the students the type of story you have just seen. Is it mystery, action, adventure, situation comedy? The list of program types in Chapter 9 may be helpful. Help the students determine what makes one category of show different from another. It is, of course, this analysis that is important and not the specific categories used. Have the students decide what kinds of characters are needed for each type of program, i.e. which types need villains, funny people, serious people, and the like.

Ask the students to write the story line for the segments used and to identify the setting, the characters, and the motivating elements. Consider the solution offered by the writer. Have the students discuss how the solution was motivated and what other solutions are possible.

Prepare a dramatic script of one of the segments with the students as was done with the short story; cast, present, and record it. Compare the class version with the original and discuss the differences. This comparison is a good opportunity to consider the effect of setting.

ANALYSIS OF HOME-VIEWED MATERIALS. Ask the students to be prepared to analyze a favorite program they will view at home on a chosen evening. Ask them to think about program type, major and minor characters, the story line, and motivating elements. Each student should jot down these observations. The program analysis form in the workbook section may be adapted for these purposes. The next day, discuss the programs viewed in terms of the items listed. Ask the students to decide what kinds of problems are usually presented in each of the series represented and to determine whether the specific program viewed was typical of the series. Talk about personal choices to the extent that students are able to become aware of the selection process.

One word of caution: Any viewing assignment at home has to fit in with the household rules governing the use of the television set. It will not be unusual in a class of thirty to find one or two students who do not have access to television during the week or at all. When motivating the students to view, be sure to leave room for the student who cannot. On the other hand, the transfer of the skills learned in the classroom to the home viewing situation is vital to the success of this curriculum. We have found no better way to aid this transfer than home viewing assignments. You can enlist the student in this transfer process by having them discuss the differences they felt in doing the tasks at home as compared with doing them in the classroom.

Prepare a classroom/home-viewing exercise. Record an early

evening entertainment program that is part of a continuing series. View the program in class, focusing on characters and characterization. The character analysis form in the workbook section may be useful. In addition, the students might approach the following questions:

- Who were the main characters?
- How could you tell who the main characters were?
- How were the characters expressed in what they did and what they said?
- Which characters would you like to know? To have as friends or neighbors?
- What did the characters do that you agreed with? Disagreed with?

Discussion of the answers to these questions should take place on the day the program series is regularly scheduled. After the discussion, assign the program for home viewing (again it will be necessary to allow for individual family rules). Have the students address the same questions as those used in the classroom viewing. Ask these in addition:

- What new characters were introduced in this episode?
- Did the repeating characters change? Was there any progression evident?
- Do we now have new information about the repeating characters that would allow us to enlarge our description of them?
- What was the same? Uninteresting? Repetitious?
    Repeat this two step exercise but focus on plot conflict. These questions might be useful:
- What was the conflict used to motivate the action?
- What would the plot have been like if the conflict(s) had been left out?
- Were the conflicts settled in sensible ways?
- What alternate solutions were available?
- How would similar conflicts be settled in real life?
- What knowledge or beliefs did you have to suspend in order to enjoy this program?

For the home viewing portion repeat the above questions and add:

- Were the conflicts for this episode drawn from the same formula?

- How were they the same? How were they different?
- Were the solutions drawn from the same formula?
- How were they the same? How were they different?

EXERCISES IN REALITY TESTING. Using the videotaped entertainment segments, have the students identify which actions are good approximations of reality and which are not. Help them to determine the utility of realism in certain types of programs. Discuss where realism will not work. Saturday morning cartoons and superhero programs will be particularly useful to demonstrate the value of fantasy.

Select one of the segments that shows an activity or occupation about which additional information can be gathered from different sources. Gather that information and compare it to the televised information. Introduce the notion of dramatic intent and the fact that a dramatic author has no responsibility to properly represent reality.

EXERCISES IN DESCRIBING PRODUCTION VALUES. Help the student develop a glossary of descriptive terms for sights and sounds. The workbook section has lists appropriate to sound and visual images. Work with the camera to develop the notion of the camera shot as analogous to the sentence. Shots are put together to form scenes just as sentences form paragraphs. Discuss the concept of shot progression as scenes develop from wide angle views or establishing shots to tighter and tighter views of the specific action. Transitions between scenes go back to the establishing shot. Look at the impact of the close-up. It is television's most dramatic shot.

Make arrangements to visit the local television station. While most stations do not produce their own dramatic shows, many visual and auditory effects are produced for the news program. The station will usually be willing to demonstrate visual effects like matting, superimpositions, shot progression, and camera perspective on their news set. There are a number of short films that show how movies accomplish different effects; some may be available in your film catalogue.

The construction of an entertainment program becomes readily transparent with a note sheet and a watch. Either in the classroom or as a home viewing assignment have the students observe the temporal structure of the program. The placement of commercials will give good guideposts to mark the development of plot. With a bit of practice the students will readily recognize the basic form of a short introductory phase preceding the opening commercial, followed by a longer middle phase that establishes the problem or conflict to be solved, which will end in a moment of suspense just prior to the middle commercial break. The third phase will build to the climax, which will occur just prior to the final commercial break. After that break the program will return to disentangle the last of the loose ends. Students can be asked to time each of these phases and to note the ebb and flow·of action within the phases. This exercise also provides an opportunity to time the length of the breaks and to note the number of different commercial messages that are presented.

ANALYSIS OF SERIES THEMES, PLOTS, AND STORY LINES. Hand out the forms for series analysis that are provided in the workbook section. Have each student select an entertainment series that is viewed frequently. Ask them to do the series analysis of what they recall. Ask the children to jot down in a few lines a description that will tell what to expect from programs in a series such as *The Waltons, Little House on the Prairie* or any other. Ask the students to describe the kinds of conflicts and resolutions that generally occur in the series they have analyzed. Have the students describe a typical plot, the continuing characters, and their motivations.

The differences between themes, story lines, and plots may be difficult for the younger viewers to grasp, especially if the focus is upon memorizing the terms. Instead, approach the meanings of these three terms by asking students to think about a statement they could write that would tell the kind of problems and actions that usually occur in a specific TV series. After they have tried this exercise, have them share their statements. Once they understand what they have done, tell them that they have been telling the repeated themes for a particular program. They may want to look up the dictionary definition after they have been guided through their own operational definition.

Do the same type of thing with story line and plot. To develop a working understanding of story line, ask the students to write a sentence or two telling what a TV program was about but avoiding telling about the problems and characters. An understanding of plot can be approached by asking students to write a paragraph that will tell about the conflicts that led to character action in a program, how the conflicts were settled, and what became of the main characters.

Obviously, this activity may involve discussion and writing activity over a period of several days. It can be related to ongoing work in expository writing. It can use the stories that the students are reading in reading class as the material for story line and plot identification.

ANALYSIS OF ROLE AND OCCUPATION MODELS. Have students identify TV characters that people their age would like to be like. Encourage them to describe the characteristics that are particularly admirable. Have the students consider the consequences of being like that character — what the individual could and could not do. Consider the advantages and disadvantages of other role models.

Analysis of occupational role models can be accomplished through use of videotape entertainment programs that show common occupations such as, policeman, teacher, reporter. Have someone who actually holds that occupation view the appropriate segment with the class and discuss the differences between how an occupation is shown on TV and how it is in actuality.

EXTENDED ACTIVITIES

1. Note the different kinds of entertainment programs (mystery, action, adventure, etc.). List the characteristics of each kind of program. Determine which characteristics are essential to that type of program and which are secondary. Which characteristics appear in more than one type of program?

2. Develop a worksheet that could be used to help children recognize parts of the story line as it is developed between commercial interruptions during a 30 minute program.

3. After identifying the main characters of a weekly program, list the actions those characters are involved in over a two or three week period. Classify those actions as desirable or undersirable. Discuss how your attitude toward the main characters would change if their behavior were to change.

4. Tape (video, if possible) a ten minute segment from a popular television show. Prepare a script from the tape. When the class is familiar with the script (through reading it and listening to it), have them write in the stage directions for the segment. Only after they have prepared their own stage directions should they see the visual portion of the tape.

5. Tape a ten minute segment from a popular television show (as

in above). Show the class the video and keep the audio silent. Have the class prepare the script. When it is polished to their satisfaction, allow them to watch the tape with both audio and video.

6. After concluding the two previous activities, discuss which was easier to do; which came closer to approximating the taped segment; which medium carries more of the information (character develop, plot, etc.); which medium may be subordinate to the other.

Workbook Section
for Entertainment Content

LIST OF DESCRIPTIVE WORDS
FOR
SOUND AND VISUAL IMAGES

In order to give you some help in describing what goes on during a television program, we asked people who work in television to give us a list of special words they use to describe the pictures and sound they produce. These two lists are reproduced below. The first list gives the words used to describe the quality, both artistic and technical, of the sounds that you hear. The second is the list of words used to describe picture quality. It is not necessary that you know *all* these words. However, if you get stuck in answering the program guide or the series guide for a word to describe what you saw or heard, these lists will always be handy.

SOUND IMAGES		*VISUAL IMAGES*	
loud	touching	bright	has depth
soft	sensuous	dim	beautiful
harsh	bleak	indistinct	moving
harmonious	eerie	happy	dynamic
bright	noisy	colorful	pleasing
intense	clean	drab	typical
clear	fidelity	intense	confused
garbled	resonance	ugly	lovely
raspy	beat	appealing	clear
grating	blunt	repulsive	in focus
rumbling	crisp	unfocused	high clarity
hollow	muted	multicolored	pastorial
nasal	distorted	pretty	strong
light	discordant	sharp	vivid
capturing	dead	fuzzy	soft
irritating	diffused	opaque	slick
ringing	reverberated	contrasty	color
echoing	precise	washed out	light
shrill	motivated	negative	massive
soothing	counterpointing	outline	delicate
muddy	reinforcing	detailed	solid
busy	stinging	radiant	liquid
off mike	distracting	misty	fluid
buzzing	underscoring	foggy	close-up

SOUND IMAGES *(continued)*

smooth	realistic		
continuous	symbolic		
pleasing	rhythmic		
disruptive	jangly		
uncomfortable	sharp		
blurry	sleepy		
flat	graceful		
contrasty	forceful		
balanced	strident		
lifelike	sloppy		
funny	slick		
sad	professional		
swooping	amateur		
gliding	brassy		
climbing	cool		
shocking	hot		
startling	sunny		
quick	chopped up		
peppy			

VISUAL IMAGES *(continued)*

flat	wide shot
bland	half tone
has snap	balance
noisy	symmetrical
busy	asymmetrical
graphic	busy
linear	sparse
diffused	cold
symbolic	silhouette
striking	elegant
patterned	dense
formal	blurry
stylistic	flat
looks posed	lifelike
poetic	cool
pastel	hot
surreal	double exposure
impressionistic	reversed polarity

PROGRAM ANALYSIS GUIDE

1. Briefly, what was the story about?

2. What were the major themes? Look at the theme categories listed below. Determine which themes were used in the program you saw. A program might be all one theme or might contain more than one. Check all themes that were used. Determine how much time was spent on the development of each theme. Give the theme that was developed the most a score of "1"; the next one a "2"; and so on.

Check If Used	*Development Score*	*THEME*
_____	_____	COMEDY — Situations were developed that would support dialogue and/or action designed for humor.
_____	_____	ACTION/VIOLENCE — Situations were presented that depicted crime, war, and/or individuals attacking others.
_____	_____	ACTION/DANGER — Situations were developed where one or more characters were in danger of injury or death due to the elements, terrain, disease, or other nonhuman causes.
_____	_____	DRAMA/DANGER — Situations were presented where the characters were threatened with the loss of something held important (e.g., reputation, job, money, fame) but not with personal injury or death.
_____	_____	DRAMA/SLICE OF LIFE — Series is of a continuing nature with this program presenting the characters interacting in "ordinary" or "every-day" situations.

3. Who were the characters? What role did they play (who were they)?

Name   *Role*

4. How are the major characters portrayed? Write the name of the most important character at the top of the first column; then, check all the words that would describe the character (not the actor). Write the name of the next most important character in the second column and check the words that apply. Continue until you run out of space of characters. Be sure to use only those characters who regularly appear in the series.

Name_____	Name_____	Name_____	Name_____	Name_____
Pleasant	Pleasant	Pleasant	Pleasant	Pleasant
Kind	Kind	Kind	Kind	Kind
Warmhearted	Warmhearted	Warmhearted	Warmhearted	Warmhearted
Friendly	Friendly	Friendly	Friendly	Friendly
Hard	Hard	Hard	Hard	Hard
Cool	Cool	Cool	Cool	Cool
Loud	Loud	Loud	Loud	Loud
Aggressive	Aggressive	Aggressive	Aggressive	Aggressive
Relaxed	Relaxed	Relaxed	Relaxed	Relaxed
Beautiful	Beautiful	Beautiful	Beautiful	Beautiful
Handsome	Handsome	Handsome	Handsome	Handsome
Romantic	Romantic	Romantic	Romantic	Romantic
Dynamic	Dynamic	Dynamic	Dynamic	Dynamic
Rebellious	Rebellious	Rebellious	Rebellious	Rebellious
Self-centered	Self-centered	Self-centered	Self-centered	Self-centered
Whiney	Whiney	Whiney	Whiney	Whiney
Fearful	Fearful	Fearful	Fearful	Fearful
Suspicious	Suspicious	Suspicious	Suspicious	Suspicious
Rough exterior	Rough exterior	Rough exterior	Rough exterior	Rough exterior
Cold exterior	Cold exterior	Cold exterior	Cold exterior	Cold exterior
Righteous	Righteous	Righteous	Righteous	Righteous

Name_____	Name_____	Name_____	Name_____	Name_____
Mean	Mean	Mean	Mean	Mean
Abrasive	Abrasive	Abrasive	Abrasive	Abrasive
Docile	Docile	Docile	Docile	Docile
Compliant	Compliant	Compliant	Compliant	Compliant
Slow	Slow	Slow	Slow	Slow
Foolish	Foolish	Foolish	Foolish	Foolish
Dull	Dull	Dull	Dull	Dull
Bright	Bright	Bright	Bright	Bright
Witty	Witty	Witty	Witty	Witty
Sad	Sad	Sad	Sad	Sad
Strong	Strong	Strong	Strong	Strong
Brave	Brave	Brave	Brave	Brave
Cruel	Cruel	Cruel	Cruel	Cruel
Honest	Honest	Honest	Honest	Honest
Mature	Mature	Mature	Mature	Mature
Wise	Wise	Wise	Wise	Wise
Calm	Calm	Calm	Calm	Calm
Proud	Proud	Proud	Proud	Proud
Gentle	Gentle	Gentle	Gentle	Gentle
Violent	Violent	Violent	Violent	Violent
Happy	Happy	Happy	Happy	Happy
Ugly	Ugly	Ugly	Ugly	Ugly
Bland	Bland	Bland	Bland	Bland
Humble	Humble	Humble	Humble	Humble
Generous	Generous	Generous	Generous	Generous
Cowardly	Cowardly	Cowardly	Cowardly	Cowardly

5. What were the issues of conflict or the situations to be resolved?

6. What were the methods used to resolve the conflicts or situations?

7. What was the resolution of each issue or situation?

8. Describe the scene that was most interesting to you. What was the action? How would you describe the picture and sound?

Were any special effects or "tricks" used?

9. If the story was a drama rather than a comedy, was it believable? What didn't seem true to life?

10. If the story was a comedy, what worked best to make it funny — the characters, the situations or the dialogue?

11. Would you like to see a program like this one again? Why?

12. Were any special effects or "tricks" used? Describe them.

SERIES ANALYSIS GUIDE

1. Briefly describe the kind of story that would be typical of this series.

2. What major themes frequently appear in the stories of this series? Look at the categories listed below. Determine which themes seem to best describe the stories that usually appear. Give the most common theme a score of "1" and the next "2" and so on. If a theme is not used, score it zero.

Use Score   THEME

_____   COMEDY — Situations are developed that would support dialogue and/or action designed for humor.

_____   ACTION/VIOLENCE — Situations are presented that depict crime, war, and/or individuals attacking others.

_____   ACTION/DANGER — Situations are developed where one or more characters are commonly in danger of injury or death due to the elements, terrain, disease or other nonhuman causes.

_____   DRAMA/DANGER — Situations are presented where the characters are commonly threatened with the loss of something held important (e.g. reputation, job, money, game) but not with personal injury or death.

_____   DRAMA/SLICE OF LIFE — Series is of a continuing story nature with programs presenting one more day in or incident in the lives of the characters.

3. Who are the repeating characters? What roles do they play?

Name   *Role*

4. How were the characters portrayed? Write the name of the most important character at the top of the first column; then, check all the words that would describe the character (not the real person or actor). Then write the name of the next most important character in the second column and check the words that apply. Continue until you run out of space of characters.

Name_____	Name_____	Name_____	Name_____	Name_____
Pleasant	Pleasant	Pleasant	Pleasant	Pleasant
Kind	Kind	Kind	Kind	Kind
Warmhearted	Warmhearted	Warmhearted	Warmhearted	Warmhearted
Friendly	Friendly	Friendly	Friendly	Friendly
Hard	Hard	Hard	Hard	Hard
Cool	Cool	Cool	Cool	Cool
Loud	Loud	Loud	Loud	Loud
Aggressive	Aggressive	Aggressive	Aggressive	Aggressive
Relaxed	Relaxed	Relaxed	Relaxed	Relaxed
Beautiful	Beautiful	Beautiful	Beautiful	Beautiful
Handsome	Handsome	Handsome	Handsome	Handsome
Romantic	Romantic	Romantic	Romantic	Romantic
Dynamic	Dynamic	Dynamic	Dynamic	Dynamic
Rebellious	Rebellious	Rebellious	Rebellious	Rebellious
Self-centered	Self-centered	Self-centered	Self-centered	Self-centered
Whiney	Whiney	Whiney	Whiney	Whiney
Fearful	Fearful	Fearful	Fearful	Fearful
Suspicious	Suspicious	Suspicious	Suspicious	Suspicious
Rough exterior	Rough exterior	Rough exterior	Rough exterior	Rough exterior
Cold exterior	Cold exterior	Cold exterior	Cold exterior	Cold exterior
Righteous	Righteous	Righteous	Righteous	Righteous
Mean	Mean	Mean	Mean	Mean
Abrasive	Abrasive	Abrasive	Abrasive	Abrasive
Docile	Docile	Docile	Docile	Docile
Compliant	Compliant	Compliant	Compliant	Compliant
Slow	Slow	Slow	Slow	Slow
Foolish	Foolish	Foolish	Foolish	Foolish
Dull	Dull	Dull	Dull	Dull
Bright	Bright	Bright	Bright	Bright
Witty	Witty	Witty	Witty	Witty

Name_____	Name_____	Name_____	Name_____	Name_____
(continued)				
Sad	Sad	Sad	Sad	Sad
Strong	Strong	Strong	Strong	Strong
Brave	Brave	Brave	Brave	Brave
Cruel	Cruel	Cruel	Cruel	Cruel
Honest	Honest	Honest	Honest	Honest
Mature	Mature	Mature	Mature	Mature
Wise	Wise	Wise	Wise	Wise
Calm	Calm	Calm	Calm	Calm
Proud	Proud	Proud	Proud	Proud
Gentle	Gentle	Gentle	Gentle	Gentle
Violent	Violent	Violent	Violent	Violent
Happy	Happy	Happy	Happy	Happy
Ugly	Ugly	Ugly	Ugly	Ugly
Bland	Bland	Bland	Bland	Bland
Humble	Humble	Humble	Humble	Humble
Generous	Generous	Generous	Generous	Generous
Cowardly	Cowardly	Cowardly	Cowardly	Cowardly

5 . What do you think the people who watch this series like about this series?

6. What do you think people might dislike about this series?

INSTRUCTIONS FOR A BRETZ BOX

Rudy Bretz, author, teacher, and television innovator, devised a simple viewing box that reproduces the effects of a camera lens' angle of view. By looking through this box one can get an excellent idea of the unique perspective of a camera. Instructions for building the box follow. Please read them all the way through first. Small errors in measuring the dimensions of the box will not affect its performance.

Materials needed: Poster board, ruler in 16ths, masking tape, utility knife or single edged razor blade.

1. Start with six pieces of poster board all six inches square. One side of the board should be black or dark colored.

2. Set two pieces aside for the top and the bottom.

3. On side 1 cut out a rectangle 3 1/2 inches wide by 2 and 5/8 inches high. The rectangle will be centered if you leave 1 and 3/4 inch margins on each side and 1 and 11/16 inches margins top and bottom. To work best all the cut-outs must be centered. On the top margin of the light colored side, write, "90 mm lens."

4. On side 2 cut out a rectangle 2 and 1/4 inches wide by 1 and 11/16 inches high. The rectangle will be centered with 1 and 7/8 inch side margins and 2 and 5/32 inch margins top and bottom. On the top margin, light side write, "135 mm lens."

5. On side 3 cut out a rectangle 2 inches wide by 1 and 1/2 inches high. Leave side margins of 2 inches and top and bottom margins of 2 and 1/4 inches. Write, "50 mm lens" on the top margin light side.

6. On side 4 cut out a rectangle 1 and 3/8 inches wide by 1 inch high. Center the rectangle with margins of 2 and 5/16 inches on the side and 2 and 1/2 inches top and bottom. On the top margin, light side, write, "75 mm lens."

7. To start the assembly of the box hold side 1 upright with the title "90 mm lens" facing you. With masking tape join the left hand side of

side 2 to the right hand side of side 1; join the left hand side 3 to the right hand side of 2 and join side 4 to the right hand side of 3. Tape on the top and bottom. Your Bretz box is finished. Of course, additional lens openings can be cut in the top and bottom. The horizontal angle of view of any lens is given by dividing the focal length (as expressed in millimeters) by 1600. The focal length is one way a lens is described (the other is "speed") and will be marked somewhere on the lens body. The longer the focal length the more narrow the angle of view. Once you have the angle of view, it is a relatively simple trigonometric problem to solve for the base of a six inch equilateral triangle (a chance for the mathematically inclined to shine). Television is in a three to four aspect ratio giving three units of height for every four units of width. Consequently the height of the rectangle cut out will be 3/4th's of the width.

The three by four aspect ratio is an important rule to keep in mind when selecting pictures or in making signs for television. Both can be any size as long as you maintain the proper aspect ratio.

Chapter 6

DEVELOPING BASIC SKILLS THROUGH THE STUDY OF TELEVISION NEWS

TELEVISION news programs have an important role in telling the stories that have always interested people. In contrast to TV entertainment content, the news program uses real events to tell the stories about "how things work," "what things are," and "choices and decisions." Fantasy and myth are not expected to dominate TV news as they do the sit-coms, police thrillers, and the soaps. Even so, the young TV viewer will need to apply skills of analysis and evaluation to the news just as he does to the commercials and entertainment programs of television.

Basic language skills that are used, and extended, in studying television news include the following:

1. Identifying relationships between the apparent intent of a message and its visual and oral content (informational, biased, propaganda).

2. Recognize the presence or absence of "source" in a news item (attribution).

3. Recognizing editorial elements, as contrasted to reportorial, in a news item.

4. Recognizing incompleteness in a news item through the formulation of questions that were not answered nor mentioned in the story.

It can be seen that these skills are basic to effective use of language, and to critical thinking. Inasmuch as television news is a one-way communication, the young viewer can not interrogate the news program concerning sources, completeness, and the like. Development and application of the skills listed above should lead the young viewer to defer this conclusion until he has consulted other media sources, such as newspapers, radio, and later TV accounts (initial TV accounts of the Reagan assassination attempt reported that Press Secretary Brady had been killed, an account that was attributed to a White House Source).

96

The long-standing inclusion of current events or contemporary affairs in the social studies curriculum has been based upon several assumptions:

1. Early experiences with the news provide attitudinal bases for a life-long interest in the public affairs of community, state, and nation.

2. Citizen participation in the processes of government requires open access to relevant information.

3. Effective use of information requires that the skills of critical analysis must be applied in assessing the credibility and meaning of any piece of public information.

4. Knowledge about the media that deliver information is essential to the complete study of the news.

In the sections that follow, these traditional social studies concerns are addressed. The information about TV news will provide an adequate background for teacher-pupil discussion. The activities that are suggested are designed to promote building of basic skills by application to the informational programs of television.

The effective use of television news and other information programs requires a combination of language and critical thinking skills. The development of critical viewing skills through the use of television news and documentaries can be integrated into the social studies curriculum, particularly in the study of contemporary affairs. However, it is necessary to do more than attend to the events of the day and the significance they may hold for the community and nation. It is necessary to understand that economic factors place many limiting conditions on television news, and to hold these conditions in mind as one views and assesses any television news program.

First, television news as an institution will be dealt with, followed by teaching activities designed to build appropriate skills. The combination of concepts, based on information, and skills, provides the basis for more effective and critical use of television news.

Television rating services report that approximately 45 percent of their respondents view one of the three network news programs, and about 40 percent watch the local news at the end of prime time. The Television Information Office continues to report that television is the primary source of news for the American adult. Television news is an important information source, but it is subject to powerful forces that can deflect it from its aim of reporting the significant events of the day. This chapter explores those forces and their effect on the news product.

TELEVISION NEWS: LOCAL STATION OPERATIONS

Television news on the local level is an extremely lucrative enterprise. News operations may generate up to half of the total income derived from local programming. It is very important, then, for a general manager to have a successful news operation. Success, as always in commercial broadcasting, is measured in ratings. In a large market the difference of one or two ratings points can translate into the gain or loss of $500,000 in yearly gross revenue. According to the current "gospel" of the market-place, ratings are generated through intense local coverage and an attractive anchor team. This section investigates how the news stories develop and the processes that lead to the selection of the anchor team.

The News Story: News Department Organization

On-line broadcast station management begins with the general manager. In commercial broadcasting he has two major purposes: (1) to maximize profit and (2) to retain the station's license. In many stations the news director will report directly to him. The news director has overall responsibility for news operation. She is responsible for budget, personnel, facilities, and final editorial decisions.

In terms of the news story, the next person in line is the assignment editor. It is the assignment editor's task to assign the stories to be covered by the reporting teams. The job sounds simple but it accounts for about half of the news we see.

One part of the job is to keep a day book in which is listed the events scheduled for that day and the reports of newsworthy occurrences that have been fed in by reporters, stringers, news releases, tips, and so on. From this list of possible stories, the assignment editor makes the initial decision on what shall be on the news on a given day. If the story is not assigned or covered in a reporter's regular beat, it will not be reported on the news programs.

The team of reporters will receive its list of assignments from the editor, who will tell them where to go, the people to contact, what the event is about, some advice on how to cover the story, and how much time will be needed for the story on the news program.

The reporting team serves two purposes: (1) to collect the factual information, which will be turned into the story reported on the air, and (2) to provide film or video tape support for the verbal report. The visual support component is an important element in determining what will go on the air and the amount of coverage the story will receive. A potent appeal of television is the ability to show the story. News programs that rely on the talking face of the anchor person have shown little success in the ratings battle. If the story cannot be covered visually, in practical terms, its likelihood of being presented is substantially reduced.

In some cases, the reporting team will turn in the verbal notes and the film or video tape to a copywriter and to a video editor, respectively. The copywriter will write a draft of the story as it might be presented. The video editor will select the shots with the most visual appeal and determine the order that will best present the story. Clearly, both the copywriter and the video editor must make judgments about the relative importance of the elements of a story although neither were present at the event.

The story, with its visual support, then goes to a person whose title may be news producer or rewrite editor. This individual assembles all the stories into the nightly report of the news. The producer/rewrite editor's prime responsibility is to make sure that the news to be presented will fit the time slot alloted for the presentation of the "hard news." Each news program has about 12 minutes to fill with news for each evening. A news program cannot extend its time as a newspaper can add pages. If there is too much news, something must be cut. Decisions have to be made on the relative importance of each story.

There are also "slow" news days. The rewrite editor will have stories, not dated by time, in storage that can be added to fill the program. Whether or not a particular story gets presented, then, often depends on the relative news load of the day on which it is collected.

Finally, in this list of persons who handle the news, are the on-air personalities. No area in news has changed so substantially as has the on-the-air presentation of the news story. On-the-air newspersons have become personalities whose interaction is a noticeable part of the presentation. The reason for this change is, again, ratings.

Interactive presentations have shown to have much greater appeal than the single, sober-sided presenter. "Happy talk" news, as this is sometimes called, has received considerable criticism, as being distracting, time-consuming, and inappropriate to the character of the news. Additionally, the complaint has been raised that the news personality has been chosen more for acting ability than the ability to cover the events of the day. It is possible that the person in whom so many viewers trust to report first hand information may not have been out of the studio at all.

The News Story: Sources — The Interview

The ordinary, one-on-one interview is a preplanned interaction between the reporter and the respondent. In most such interviews, there are no surprises, no questions that would seriously alienate the news source. Before the interview, the reporter will discuss with the respondent the subjects to be covered in the interview and the general phrasing of the questions. In some few cases, interviews in the studio may be fully rehearsed. Two other practices are also used, on occasion, to modify the actual interview: One is called sharpening. Respondents are usually accorded the courtesy of improving or sharpening an answer, if the first answer given and recorded was not satisfactory to the respondent. The second practice is the inserted reaction shot. In the process of the reporter-respondent contact, the film team will shoot unplanned shots of reporter and/or the respondent listening or reacting to some discussion perhaps unrelated to the interview. These shots are then used in the final filmed story as reactions to specific questions. The reporter in the film may show deep interest in the answer, while at the actual interview he was fooling with some piece of equipment. There have been accusations of misuse of this technique, where editorial statements have been created by "editing in" reactions that express surprise or concern with a question when this did not happen. Abuses tend to be rare, however, as the reporter may wish to interview the respondent again.

The News Story: Sources — The Reporter's Beat

Beyond covering specific assignments, the reporter also covers a "beat." The beat is in actuality a series of contacts the reporter has developed within selected areas of news.

In a given news presentation, about half of the stories will be assigned and the other half will come from the beats of reporting staff. The relationship between a news reporter and her contacts is one of mutual exchange. The news reporter uses her contact to get stories otherwise unavailable. Her contacts, on the other hand, depend on the news reporter to make sure that information, particularly the "right" information, gets known. The potential for bias is clear. Reporters can protect contacts by not reporting unfavorable news about them or they may become overly dependent on their contacts and not seek out additional sources of news. We see the effect of this mutual dependence in the relatively little investigative reporting that is conducted at the local level.

The News Story: Sources — The Press Release

Each day scores of organizations prepare statements for release to the press. Most organizations of any size maintain specific departments for that purpose. Press releases are written with purpose. They typically attempt to advance the well-being of the organization. What is somewhat surprising is how many of these releases get published in the newspaper or presented on the air with little or no action on the part of the news media. Press officers have become quite knowledgeable in preparing the release in the style and format which the medium prefers. Many will produce a complete story with film or videotape support. Some stations will run these stories without review. Others will tag the film with an identification of source (all films supplied by holders of political office must be tagged). Still other stations have a blanket policy against the use of such stories. Nevertheless, most stations make some use of "press release news."

The News Story: Sources — The Press Conference and The News Event

The press conference is an organized method of releasing news, which permits reporters to interact with the news source (usually) and to have a source of visual support. As it requires active participation by the news organization, the press conference is restricted to those instances where the information or the news source has intrinsic news worth. While the press conference is usually a step up from the press release, it is still a highly managed source of news. Probably a major impediment is the limited capacity for a reporter to follow a complete line of questions and follow-up inquiry. At large press conferences, the questioning jumps from reporter to reporter and from topic to topic. Vague or obfuscating answers cannot be clarified.

The news event is a common technique by which politicians, entertainers, and the like maintain exposure. The news event may be a speech, a party, or a dedication, a demonstration, or any visually appealing activity. Timing a news event has become quite sophisticated. In order to maximize the likelihood of coverage, the following must be provided: (1) notification of the event must, of course, be forwarded to the assignment editor in sufficient time for crews to be assigned; (2) the event itself has to be held to coincide with presentation deadlines; and (3) in the event, the appearance of the "newsmaker" has to be well scheduled for the convenience of the reporting crew. The news event is, indeed, an event for news.

The News Story: Sources — Actuality

In the make-up of news, the actuality, the actual event — unplanned, unmanaged — constitutes a relatively small percentage of the news stories, primarily because it is unplanned and unmanaged. In order for such events to be covered, a news team has to be on-site. Common actualities that are presented are fires, automobile wrecks, floods, labor stoppages, etc. It is a complaint of critics that the news tends to focus on the disaster, and on the spectacular disaster at that.

From time to time the problem of a staged actuality crops up. Usually, such accusations occur when documentary presentations need a bit of visual action to cover the text of the script. The presence of the television cameras, however, can also encourage renewed activity on the part of demonstrators and others striving for the public eye. Reporters have been known to ask "Show me what you did" or "Do it again, will ya?" Actualities are not always real.

In many cases, the actual event may be over by the time the news

team arrives. In those cases, the event is "recreated" through interviews of eye witnesses. The notion of the event thus developed is, of
course, wholly dependent on the reliability of the witnesses interviewed.

The News Story: Sources — Wire Services

There are two major wire services in the United States, United
Press International and The Associated Press. Both provide a news
service for broadcasting. The Associated Press is an organization of
associated newspaper and broadcast outlets who share their news.
Each member news organization makes a copy of each story, which
is then forwarded to the regional AP editor. The story is stored by
computer; if, in the judgment of the editor, it merits additional exposure, it is sent by regional wire (regional split) to news outlets in
the locale. A story of national interest is picked up by the national
editor for that region and sent out to all subscribers. Along the line,
the story will be rewritten by regional and national staffers. Consequently, a national story has passed through at least three layers of
editorial judgment before it reaches the public and has been rewritten several times. The potential for error rises with each of these occurrences.

The United Press International is organized as a news gathering
company. UPI has offices in most major cities and hires "stringers"
for other areas. A UPI story, then, is likely to pass through fewer
layers, but UPI has less news flow. Most national news in our
newspapers is wire service news, which appears with little more than
stylistic changes from the way it was received on the paper's teletype.
Much of radio news, both national and local, is wire service news.
Most radio stations cannot afford a news staff; consequently, the
news they present is not their own. A common derogatory description of a low budget news service is "It's a 'rip and read' operation,"
because it is torn from the teletype machine.

The News Story: Sources — The Network

In recent years, local affiliate stations have been augmenting
their news presentations, particularly their late news, with stories
developed by the national network staff. Network news works much

like Associated Press. That is, affiliate stations pass on news stories of national interest to the network which may cover the story with its own team or use the local coverage. Stories are sent down the network inter-connect and taped by the receiving station for possible later use. Stations find such stories particularly appealing because they are completely produced and can be plugged directly into the local program. Independent stations, of course would not have access to network stories, and it is quite rare that a news story from one network would be shown on another's affiliate station. The single exception to that practice is the common exchange of sports coverage such as football or basketball.

TELEVISION INFORMATION PROGRAMS: THE TALK SHOW

Television talk shows now appear in every part of the day except prime time. They are essentially of two types: (1) the entertainment show whose talk is socializing and (2) the information show whose talk is socially relevant. The entertainment based talk show is almost always in a magazine format with multiple guests, like multiple articles in a magazine. The "plugging" of guest's activities or enterprises is rampant. The information presented is not subject to analysis but is generally presented without review. The informative talk show may be of the magazine format, such as the morning programs or the very late night interviews, or an entire program may be devoted to a single subject and guest, such as the several syndicated shows now available (Mike Douglas, Phil Donahue, etc.). Information on these programs is usually subjected to some testing in question and answer or discussion. The single subject programs appear to be much more successful in exploring a subject and in providing a review of the material.

TELEVISION INFORMATION PROGRAMS: DOCUMENTARIES

The documentary is the cinemographic equivalent of the literary essay. It assembles facts, statements, and opinions to advance a particular point of view. There is usually a tone of moral concern if not outrage. The subjects selected are vulnerable, open to criticism. Documentaries are currently in two formats: (1) the extended program (usually at least 90 minutes) and (2) the documentary magazine. Extended documentaries appear infrequently, on a "special" basis. The documentary magazine has shown considerable audience appeal in the last few seasons and will be developed by each network as long as that appeal holds. The documentary is a persuasive argument, with the powerful appeal of appearing to present things as they actually are. The "objective news reporter" presentation style is typically employed to heighten the credibility of the presentation. All the elements in the analysis of the perceived reality of television entertainment programs can be applied to the analysis of television documentaries. The single exception is the dramatic intent, which allows the entertainment author the deceits necessary to progress her plot. The documentarist must not present that which is not true, but neither must she present all that is true.

A recent development in television entertainment has been the fictionalized documentary (e.g., *Roots, Holocaust*). The fictionalized documentary is analogous to the historical novel. The fictionalized documentary augments historical events and facts with an enlarged story line, broader characterizations, and the addition of motivating elements. Much of what is presented is true to fact; the difficulty is that none of it need be. Once again we have returned to a dramatic intent while remaining in a documentary form. If done properly, the result should be an overall impression that is true, but any one detail could be false. It would seem particularly important to identify this dramatic form as separate from a documentary and of a different information value.

COMPARATIVE ANALYSIS OF MEDIA NEWS

It is characteristic of different media that each will present a news story in a different way. Television tends to present the news in the present tense. It is a "what's happening now" approach to the concept of news. Newspapers, because of their less frequent appearance and greater space capacity, tend to see events in a longer perspective. The writing is in the past tense. An event will have a longer "story life" for a newspaper than it will for television news. News magazines have an even greater time perspective. Magazine reporting tends to be less concerned with the event itself than with the consequences of the event. This concern results from the obvious time span of a weekly or monthly appearance schedule.

Content also varies. Television succeeds with the visual, the immediate impact. Print has less success in reporting the intensity of a fire but can more thoroughly report the economic and social consequences. Newspapers usually perceive themselves as the area's "journal of record." As a consequence, they are more concerned with the legal and social events of the locale than either television or news magazines. News magazines tend to avoid stories of only local or regional interest or seek to interpret those stories from a wider viewpoint.

The issue of credibility often surfaces in a comparative analysis of media news. Basically it addresses the question of which medium should have greater credibility. Clearly, there is no "best" medium. Each is subject to common and particular biases that shape the news accordingly. Credibility is better invested in the number of different, confirming sources. Should there be conflicting stories, the likelihood is that the event is not well-known by any single medium, with each describing it from its own limited view. Confirmation of the event from different sources, particularly different sources with different publication schedules, give one some security that, at least, the event is somewhat less distorted.

TELEVISION INFORMATION PROGRAMS: SUMMARY

Television news and information programs have become a notable source of our view of the world around us. They have, as with all information sources, specific and definitive limitations. The dependence on a single source will always lead to a biased view. It is exceedingly important to understand the limitations of each source and to pursue a comparative analysis in the development of knowledge and opinion. We have discussed the limits of televised news and information. Others have extensively discussed the limits of print journalism. The combined understanding of these limits would appear to be a prerequisite to the processes of good citizenship.

Chapter 7

INSTRUCTIONAL OBJECTIVES
AND ACTIVITIES FOR NEWS
AND INFORMATION PROGRAMS

THREE concepts form the foundation of the instructional objectives and activities in this area: (1) Television can be a useful information source. (2) As an information source television has biases inherent in the economic structure of the industry and in production characteristics. (3) Analytical procedures can be utilized to identify and modify the effects of these biases.

INQUIRY QUESTIONS

- What is news?
- What information can news give you?
- What kinds of news programs are there?
- How does the information content differ between different news program types?
- What are other sources of news?
- How do we use people as sources of news?
- How is TV news different from newspapers, news magazines, radio news?
- Why is the "weather" news?
- How does sports information fit into the news?
- How do news people gather their information?
- How is a story written, pictures made, tape or film prepared?
- Who decides to put a story on the air, in the newspaper, in a magazine?
- How do they decide? What are their standards?
- What is the likelihood of error in TV news, the newspaper or magazine?
- How can we verify the information that is presented in the news?
- What is a talk show?
- Who selects the topics and guests?

- Would different people as guests express different ideas on the topic?
- What is a documentary?
- How is a documentary different from the news?
- Could different documentary treatments be made of the same subject matter?
- What is the difference between an actual documentary and a fictionalized documentary?

OBJECTIVES

Following is a list of the educational objectives for this content area. They are generally appropriate for middle grade level students, but teachers should gear activities in keeping with the readiness levels of any grade.

- Describe the differences that exist among the information programs: news, talk shows, documentaries, editorials.
- The student will be able to identify local news shows and network news shows on the basis of their content.
- The student will be able to identify advantages and limitations of TV news in comparison with news presented in other media.
- The student will demonstrate knowledge of the process by which TV news is gathered, edited, and presented.
- The student will understand the organization of the local television station with emphasis on the work of the news department.
- The student will be able to describe the various sources that contribute to the content of the TV news program.
- The student will participate in the process of the production of a news program.

ACTIVITIES

The content area of news and information is relatively removed from the work-a-day world of the child. Activities in this area are directed toward an introduction of the child to news and information programming. While the content of much of television news is irrelevant to the activity and responsibilities of a child, certain information programming with high entertainment values like *Wild Kingdom* or *Undersea World* can be of interest. The basic techniques of information analysis can be more easily managed in the lower grades with content of this latter sort than with the highly concentrated, rapid fire news presentations.

In the upper grades, a most important activity would involve making comparisons of the treatments of a common news story by television, newspapers, and news magazines. This comparative analysis will permit the identification of the inherent biases and limitations of each medium. An analysis of this sort could be profitably begun by having the students use the local and network news worksheets provided (along with other useful textual materials) at the end of the chapter. The newspaper will not, of course, report on all of the TV stories (interesting by itself) but several should appear.

An Introduction to News and Information. The VTR playback equipment will be needed for these awareness development activities, as will videotaped segments (about 5 minutes each) of a local news program, a network news program, a talk show, an entertainment show, and a documentary or magazine type show. Explain to the students that they will view several different kinds of television programs. After viewing each segment, they will be asked to decide whether it was news or entertainment programming. Spend some time developing the idea of a news program. Proceed to show each program type. After each showing ask the students to decide whether the segment was news, information, or entertainment. Help the students develop the reasons why they made those judgments. After all segments have been shown in this manner go back through them again asking the students to see if there is anything entertaining about the shows labeled news or information and if there is any information in the shows labeled entertainment. The students should be aided in recognizing that the TV news has an entertainment element (a growing one at that) and that entertainment programs can be information laden. Lead the class in a sharing of perceptions in this area. They will be better prepared to deal with the question: How can we tell whether the main purpose of a TV program is to inform or to entertain?

Network News and Local News. The VTR playback equipment should be available along with a videotape of a local news program or, if the local TV schedule permits, a viewing of a live local news program. Ask the students to keep track of the places where the news events occurred and to notice where the people in the news live. Younger children will have difficulty in accomplishing even this simple task, as news is quite dense in its factual presentation. It may be necessary to pause between each story to let the children process the information. Follow a discussion of this local news viewing with a viewing of five minutes of network news. Have the students work with the same information as they did with the local news. Discuss with the students the way local and network news differ. Analysis forms are available in the section at the end of the chapter. Caution: Keep in mind that most young people and many adults as well do not watch TV news on a regular basis. Approach these activities with no assumptions as to student familiarity with this type of content. Further, the aim of these exercises is not necessarily to encourage viewing. Many persons who work in information see television news as a supplemental source of information.

COLLECTING INFORMATION — USING THE TV LOG. The TV log is an interesting exercise, which will introduce the student to special uses of a newspaper. It will provide them with experience in locating information and in the use of a TV log to select programs for viewing.

Obtain, or have the students bring, the TV log section from the newspaper. Usually a Saturday or Sunday edition will have some information about each program. Assign each student the task of finding the listing for a network news program, a local news program, a talk show, and a documentary or magazine type show. Discuss with the students the variety of things, people, and events that might be learned through the viewing of the news shows and special information shows that will be available during the coming week. The selection of programs through the use of a TV log can represent a higher order of management of television use. This is a good opportunity to provide that skill.

THE TV NEWSPAPER NEWS SHOW. Several educational objectives can be effectively pursued in one comprehensive activity. This activity involves the students in constructing a television news show from the stories that appear in the newspaper. Prepare for this activity by obtaining a copy of a daily newspaper for each child, the same issue for all. The news sections only will suffice. Inform the students that only seven stories from the newspaper may be used on your TV show due to the limits of time. Ask each student to select the seven stories each would include on a TV news program. Compare and discuss the variety of student selections. Ask the students to give the reasons they selected the news stories they did. Use the opportunity to help them understand how the news editor of a TV station or network plays a big part in selecting the news we see on TV.

Select two stories and, with the children, edit them for presentation on TV. The average news story is 30 seconds in length or about 75 words long. Work with the children to decide what information will be kept and what deleted. You may wish to put special emphasis on information that can be pictured or supported by film, as that emphasis would be common to an editor's decision.

Encourage the students to think about these questions: Does the newspaper provide more information than the TV news show? Which provides more news stories? Does the newspaper carry all of the news that happens each day?

Select a story from the newspaper which is heavily descriptive — a fire, accident, etc. Have the students read the story and consider how television news would present the same story. The advantage of the visual presentation mode should be apparent. Discuss with the children the reasons TV news can be more exciting, more entertaining.

OBSERVATION GAME. Students can get a good insight into the problems of reporting by trying to reconstruct a surprise event in the classroom. For this exercise preplan an interruption of the regular class schedule. Whatever the event is to be, make a list of each action planned and copy this in sufficient numbers for each student. This "fact-list" will enable the students to see how well they did in reconstruction (of course, the teacher may have to add to the list if the unexpected occurs). After the event have the students discuss or write what they saw, then distribute the fact list. Discuss the problems of observation — different viewpoints, interpretation, and perspectives.

Have the students consider how they would make a news story out of the fact list. What facts are important for the viewer to know; what facts can be discarded? What visuals would aid in telling the story?

THE WORK OF NEWS. Inasmuch as a major objective at this level deals with an awareness of the work involved in gathering and selecting news for daily television news programs, it is recommended that the teacher make contact with a local station manager prior to the beginning of any study of the news. Several specific items to be discussed with the local station manager or news editor follow. (1) The availability of teletype news sheets that come from the wire services are excellent for class use. Day-old news copy is usually of little value to the station. This copy can be used to help students understand the selection and rewrite processes. (2) The availability of scripts for analysis. (3) The possibility of a visit by the news editor to the class to talk to the students about the procurement of news. If the arrangement is not too complex, a class visit to the local station's news department may be included, but the major objectives at this level do not require such a visit.

If a local news program is available during the school day, it is suggested that the students view a live show with the following assignment: Determine the source of each news story (wire service, local reporter, etc.) such as a city official, a school official, a business person, a state official, a news service. Keep in mind that the student may not be familiar with news stories nor with national wire services such as UPI or AP. The activity will stimulate them to think about where the news comes from. This knowledge is basic to a growing understanding of the effect that news gathering from certain sources has upon the news we get and that many important and interesting events may happen without ever making the news.

Consider the selection process. Using either the newspaper or wire copy, assign the students the task of selecting the twenty or so stories that they would select for a local news program. Discuss the basis of their selection. Have them consider visual support needed for each of their stories.

Schedule a resource person from the local TV station. Inform the students that they should decide on questions to ask. Have them prepare as if they were reporters. Assign the task of writing a news story about the visit. Discussion with the resource person should focus upon the way the local news team works to collect the news and upon the sources that are regularly contacted for news items.

COMPARATIVE ANALYSIS. Begin by introducing the students to the remaining media presentations of news: radio and the news magazine. Discuss radio as a headline service and the news magazine as an interpreter of the context of events.

Record, or view live, a local TV news program that falls within the same news day as a particular issue of the paper. Provide copies of the news section of the paper for the students and help them compare the treatment of the news by the two media. Radio news reports from the same period could also be added. Obtain copies of the weekly news magazine for the following week to see if any local story was included.

Have the students consider the process of verification of media news by seeking confirmation in other media, by seeking information from knowledgeable people, and by contacting primary sources.

MEDIA INFORMATION SOURCES. This exercise makes use of the comparative analysis, with special emphasis being placed on the newspaper. In preparation for the activity here, it is recommended that a complete copy of the daily newspaper be available for each student's use. Begin by having the students become familiar with the content of a newspaper. Help them discover the variety of stories included. Ask the students to look for news items that tell about sports, weather, farm activity, market activity, social news such as clubs and weddings, police and court news, and the many specialty columns. Have them make an estimate of the number and length of stories in each category.

Call their attention to the "hard news" items after they have completed the first assignment. The hard news is about local, state, national, and world events that involve government, business, or social movements. The point of these assignments is to build sensitivity to the wide range of information contained in a daily newspaper. At the same time, some discussion should ensue as to the information that is not there: news of everyday activities, product information, stories that appeal to children, and so forth.

After the students have gained a working concept of hard news, ask them to examine the first three pages of the daily newspaper and to count the number of news stories.

THE ENTERTAINMENT OF INFORMATION. The purpose here is to make the student aware of the fact that a great deal of information is presented in programs where the apparent purpose is to entertain the viewer. It is desirable that students be particularly critical of the sources of information in entertainment type programs because attribution of source may be absent altogether, while news programs are generally expected to cite sources of information.

Another difference that students may look for is the current importance or recency of the information included in entertainment content. *Wild Kingdom* is full of information of a timeless sort. The young viewer should be able to describe the way in which that information differs from daily news program content.

Finally, the student should be made aware of the method of presentation of entertaining information. The information is structured to build suspense and to develop a story. It is the story development that determines the organization of the information. Efficient delivery of information is not a major consideration.

These differences can be easily shown through the use of a videotape of brief segments of a news program, of a talk show, of a quiz show, and of a program such as *Wild Kingdom*.

SOURCES OF NEWS. This activity is better done after the preceding two as the students will be prepared to consider sources of news. These questions can be asked to direct student discussion: Where do the reporters get the news? How do they know whom to call? Where to go?

Arrange for a visit from a resource person from the television station and from the newspaper on consecutive days if possible. Have them respond to questions and describe their work. Have the students prepare to act as reporters and assign a news story to be written about the visits.

PRODUCING THE TELEVISION NEWS PROGRAM. Producing the television news program with news of the school can be particularly successful. Many skills will be practiced in the identification of news, the collection of news from the various news sources, the writing of the story, providing visual support for the story, and in its presentation. A production checklist and a team analysis form are presented in the workbook section of this chapter. Advice on in-school productions is provided in Chapter 8.

To make use of the entire class, divide the group into teams of five or six. Assign a subject area to each team, such as school administration, athletics, drama, and so forth. If the larger community can be used, look for subject areas of high interest to the students. Each team should work to develop an understanding of the subject area before gathering the news. What is the importance of the area to the audience? Who are the news sources? What kind of visual support is available? What do I need to know about the background to get the story?

It goes without saying that the cooperation of the news sources should be gained in advance. Student reporters can be surprisingly good, sometimes embarrassingly so. Nevertheless, there is a real excitement in this exercise and a great learning potential.

Workbook Section

For News and Information Programs

THE NEWS PROGRAM: SELECTION PROCESSES

The news programs that are produced by local television stations usually contain at least three parts — hard news, the weather, and the sports. Some local stations will include a brief section on community events; sometimes a local station will include a section on financial news, about the stock market and local business happenings. A special feature or human interest section may be a regular part of a local television news. Special features present stories about unusual and interesting people and places.

There may be other sections included in some local station news programs, but these six parts are the most popular. You can use this activity to prepare pupils for doing the school news show.

Selecting the News (Local News)

The local news program is different from the network news in several important ways. First, the local station does not have as many reporters and cameramen. The local station wants to cover only the local and state news so it does not need as many reporters and cameramen as the networks; still the local station must decide where to send its cameramen and reporters.

Here is a list of "events" that were reported in a medium sized city newspaper for one day. Work with your TV news team (4-5 students) to decide which of these news items you would include on your evening news program. *You will have time for only 290-320 seconds of news items because you have a lot of commercial slots on this newscast.* Notice the time that each story will take. Some have films or still photos.

1. Fire destroys an empty barn (20 seconds, film).
2. City police get new cars (30 seconds, film).
3. Homeowners to pay more taxes next year (30 seconds).
4. Amtrak passenger service to start next month (30 seconds, photos).
5. High school basketball team loses fifth straight game (30

seconds, film).
6. Governor to speak in city next week (30 seconds, photos).
7. March of Dimes' chairperson is named (20 seconds, photos).
8. Three deer seen on edge of city (20 seconds, photos of area).
9. Runaway truck smashes into gas station (30 seconds, film).
10. New factory may be located here (30 seconds, photos).
11. Mayor attends meeting in Washington, D.C. (30 seconds, photos).
12. Boy Scouts plan winter camp-out (30 seconds, film).
13. New minister for Methodist church (20 seconds, photos).
14. Two streets will get new pavement (20 seconds).
15. City's oldest resident dies at age 95 (20 seconds, photos).
16. Local housewives to protest rising grocery prices (40 seconds, film).
17. Middle school students name teacher of the year (30 seconds, photos).

Write down the number of each news item that your team will use on its news program. Give the reason why you chose each story.

Interesting class discussion can result from comparing the selections of each team and the reasons for their choices.

Number   *Time*   *We picked this because:*

_____Time total

AN ANALYSIS OF LOCAL AND NETWORK NEWS
(Written for use by students 10-12 years)

Most school age people do not watch the news very much. Yet, everyone seems to get along pretty well without it. So, what is it all about? Let us take a scientific look at the news by carefully analyzing what the news presents.

We know that there are two kinds of news programs: local news and network news. We know the local news is produced by our television stations in or near where we live. This local news is supposed to tell us the things we need to know about what is happening in our city, the cities around us, and the state in which we live. Network news, on the other hand, is produced in New York (usually) by each television network and sent to our television stations for broadcast to us. Network news specializes in what is going on in the nation and in the world. Network news tells us things that everybody in the United States might want to know.

In this activity, we want to find out how you would rate the job the network news and your local news programs are doing. We have provided an analysis form for the local programs and for the network programs. Because each local television station and each network produces its own news show, you will probably want to form teams of three or four and assign each team a particular program. It is very interesting to analyze all the news on the same day as different news producers select different stories to present. If you all analyze the same day but different programs you can compare the programs with one another.

How To Do It

News programs go by very quickly. On the average, a story lasts less than a minute. If you are not a regular viewer of news, you might want to watch a program or two before you complete the analysis form to get a "feel" of the action. You can then see how the "format" (the way it is laid out) of the program fits the format of the analysis sheet.

As you are watching, try and put the subject of the story in three or four words. The lead sentence (first one) of a story is supposed to tell you all the basic information of the story. The other sentences fill in the details. Listen closely to that first sentence for the subject matter. Many news stories will be supported by motion picture film or remote video tape. Some might have photos or charts to help give the information. Others will be told just by the news man in the studio. You will see that we have asked you to note which stories were supported by films or photos. Many news directors do not like stories told only by the news man. Sometimes, they will select a story with film and/or "kill" (not show) a story without film. Recording whether or not film was used will help you compare different news programs.

News programs compete for audiences just like entertainment programs, as they make money on the number of people they deliver to the sponsors. As a result, the program producers work to present an interesting set, perhaps some gimmicks like "action" weather or "radar" weather, and lively personalities presenting the news. All of these efforts impact on the information you receive. Maybe you will be able to see how the style of the program affects the content of the program.

One last word, our forms are designed to help you analyze the news. But if they get in the way of your analysis, figure out your own method of recording what you saw and heard. Then be ready to share your ideas with your classmates.

Study the Local News

Local News Program on Station _____
Date _____ Time of Day _____
How long was the program? _____
Hard news section: What were the news stories about? Mark a F if it had film support, a P if there were photos or charts.

1.

2.

3.

4.

5.

6.

7.

8.

Was there a weather story? Were there film or photos in it?

Was there a sports section? What were the sports stories about? Mark a F for film, a P for photos.

1.

2.

3.

Was a special features (human interest) section included? What was it about?

What else was included in the news program?

How many different persons presented news on the local station news programs?

Studying the Network News

News Program on ____ ____ ____ Network

               ABC CBS NBC

Viewed on station _____ at _____ on _____

                                   Time   Date

What were the stories about? Mark a F for film; a P for photos.

1.

2.

3.

4.

5.

6.

7.

8.

9.

10.

Which of the stories that you listed were hard news? Sports? Special
features? Weather? Business and Financial? Just use letters to
show the type of story — HN = Hard news; Sp = sports;
SF = special feature; W = weather; B = business; O = other
Were there any other stories or parts of the network news program?
Explain.

PRODUCING A NEWS PROGRAM

Chapter 8 gives some hints on how to produce your own news program. Here is a checklist to help you in planning and producing your TV news show.

1. Is your news team large enough to do all the things necessary? (5 or 6)＿＿
2. Has a news program director been chosen for each team?＿＿
3. Does everyone understand what the duties of the director are?＿＿
4. What will your news program contain? Hard news ＿＿ Weather ＿＿ Sports ＿＿ Editorial ＿＿ Business ＿＿ Special Feature ＿＿ Other ＿＿
5. Has the team decided where it will get the stories for the show?

6. How many minutes are allowed for your news program? ＿＿＿＿＿＿

7. About how much time, in seconds, do you want to give to each news item on the program?＿＿＿＿＿
8. What will you do for pictures, charts, and other visuals for the show?

9. Have the news stories been checked by the director?＿＿
10. Has the team rehearsed once before going on camera?＿＿

IN-SCHOOL NEWS PROGRAM ANALYSIS

You have worked on a news team in your class. You have helped to write and produce a news program, which has been recorded on videotape. Now you will have a chance to view the news programs that the other news teams have made. How will you decide on the quality of the news program?

1. Were the news stories important to a lot of people?

2. Which news stories were not important at all?

3. Were pictures (and other visuals) used?

4. Was the news interesting?

5. Were any of the news stories exciting or just fun to watch?

6. Were some of the news stories too long?

7. Could you understand what the reporters were saying?

After each news program that you view, write your opinion. It may go like this: "I thought this news program was good because . . . ." "I think it could be even better if these changes were made . . . ."

Chapter 8

IN SCHOOL PRODUCTIONS: PUTTING SKILLS TO WORK

EQUIPMENT

ONLY three pieces of equipment are needed to produce television programs: the camera, the microphone, and the videotape recorder. With these three pieces of equipment and adequate light, you can do a good job of production. There is some other equipment that is useful to have. For example, light sources are useful. These instruments could be photographic flood lights, lights from the theatre, or just a spot or flood light bulb screwed into a regular lamp. Easels are quite useful for holding title cards or pictures. A big roll of masking tape will be good to have on hand.

Lighting

One of the major concerns in producing television shows is lighting. We will first discuss the theory of lighting for television and then see how we can use this information in the classroom. When we light an object or person for television, we try to do so from three angles. We place one light above and behind the person. One light goes above and to the right of the person; and the third light goes above and to the left of the person. The light coming from behind the person serves to separate the person from the background. Television produces a two-dimensional picture, so if we want to show the three dimensions of distance and space we will have to do it with light. The lights to the right and left of the individual are like the sun. The sun is overhead (and so are the lights) and to the side most of the time (we turn ourselves away from facing directly into the sun). One light, either the right or the left, should be brighter than the other. This light is called the key light and it represents the light that comes from the sun. The other is not so bright and represents the light from the sun that is reflected off of the ground, buildings, and other objects onto the person's face. We can add a fourth light to soften the contrast or shadows. That light is a flood light with a broad beam and is called a fill light. Its purpose is to fill in the dark areas left by the shadows. We want to leave some shadows to show dimension and depth, but deep dark shadows are usually not an effect that we want.

We must now introduce that theory into the classroom where we might be producing our program tapes. In the simplest situation where we have no lighting instruments other than the overhead lighting and the windows, what can we do? First, it is better to work in the center of the room rather than next to one of the walls. If you cannot separate the people from the background with lights, you will have to do it with distance. Position the camera so that the light from the windows comes over the cameraman's shoulders. It is very difficult to get good pictures if the camera faces the windows (of course, you can violate all the rules and still get pictures that serve your purpose).

If you have just one lighting instrument, use it as a key light by placing it above and to the right or the left. If you have two instruments, use one as a key and other as a back light. Remember, your regular overhead lighting will serve very nicely as the fill light.

Sound

Ranking with lighting in importance is sound. Television is not only pictures but it is also the sounds — of people talking, of music, of the action. To find out how important sound is, watch your favorite program with the sound turned all the way down. It will be a lot less enjoyable. Getting good coverage of the sounds of the dialogue and action is sometimes quite difficult. The microphone, the sound receiver, is limited in ability to pick up sounds. When working from a simple set up, you usually have just one microphone. That limitation means you will have to restrict the number of people speaking so each speaker can get close enough to the microphone. Sometimes a large group can be adequately covered by sticking the microphone straight up from a desk or floor stand, or hanging it straight down from the ceiling in the center of the group. Of course, the group members must talk "to" the microphone, not to one another.

If you are doing a presentation that calls for "voice-over" sound, you can record the sound on an audio tape recorder and then play it back directly into the videotape recorder through the tape/phono jack. You can also record it through the microphone, but you may pick up unwanted noises that way.

If you have only one microphone, you will have to plan for the sound pick up carefully. Begin by limiting the number of people or other sound sources that will be "on" at any given time. Then, plan to restrict their movement to the area the microphone can cover. Practice transferring the microphone from person to person. Hand-held microphones are common, and if the transfer is done smoothly, no distraction results. Whatever you do, do not have someone talk if they cannot be "heard" by the microphone. The results will be very disappointing. Planning, as we shall see, can give the simplest presentation an effect of sophistication.

PLANNING AND REHEARSAL

Putting a television show together, even a simple one, requires the coordination of several people — the cameraman, the sound man, the videotape recorder operator, the actors, and so forth. An attempt to reach this coordination without planning and rehearsal is not likely to succeed. First, you will need a script that contains the dialogue and the major action of the actors. A shot list will have to be prepared for the cameraman so that he will know what pictures he should cover during each part of the action. Planning also includes preparing any art work (title cards, signs, pictures, etc.) to be used. If you need props (things held in the hand or placed in the setting) or special set pieces, now is the time to find them.

Once the planning is done, rehearsal begins. The first rehearsal will include just the actors. They need to practice their lines and to be blocked into their action (told where to stand and move). You will need a blocking director to do this. Remember, the director's word is law. He or she should listen to all the suggestions, but there is only one vote — the director's.

Once the actors feel reasonably comfortable with their roles, the technical rehearsal begins. This rehearsal is for the benefit of the cameraman, sound man, and videotape operator. It is not for the benefit of the actors. They must patiently repeat the scenes until everything is just right. The technical people also have a director. He may be the same person who was the blocking director, but not necessarily. The studio director works with the problems of taping what the actors will present. He does not change the actor's dialogue or action. If he has an unsolvable problem involving dialogue or action, he calls in the blocking director to make the changes.

When everybody feels comfortable with what they are supposed to do and all the technical problems have been solved, then it is time for a dress rehearsal. The dress rehearsal is just like the real thing. You should even tape it if possible. The rehearsal is played back before the crew and actors so that they can see the results and . perhaps make minor improvements. There should be no major changes now unless something is impossible. A major change should be followed by another dress rehearsal. Then, one deep breath and your show is on. We will take a quick look at the different kinds of television programs you might want to try.

KINDS OF PROGRAMS

The Commercial

Commercial production begins with a marketing plan for a specific product. What is it you are going to sell? To what target audience do you want to appeal? How can you get the people to buy? What kind of person or under what circumstances would a person have an interest in your product? What can the product do? What problems can it solve for people? Most commercials show their products as solving a problem, whether dandruff, odor, or unlovely teeth. Other commercials promise or suggest success in friendship, status, respect, or other areas where we might feel insecure.

Research Your Audience

Having decided on the product and the qualities it will have, do a little research. Talk to members of the target audience. Find out what their problems are in the area where the product works.

Scripts and Story Boards

Your research ought to help you determine the approach to take to sell your product. When you have decided on an approach you will need to develop a script. Television scripts are usually laid out in two columns. The audio side is on the right and takes up about two-thirds of the width of the paper. The video side takes up the remaining one-third on the left. The audio side has all the dialogue and sounds that occur. The video side gives a short description of each shot or picture. Once the script is written, it is a good idea to do a story board. A story board is a series of photographs or drawings, each representing a scene from the commercial. Under each frame or picture is the dialogue or sound that goes with the picture. The story board lets everyone see exactly what the commercial will be like. It is much simpler to make changes on a story board than when you are in rehearsal.

Try Something New

The first few times you make commercials you will probably want to make them like the ones you see on television. After you get some experience, try to develop some new approaches to the problem of selling. You have some restrictions: (a) you are limited to less than a minute of time — most commercials are in the ten to thirty second range; (b) your viewers must end up knowing what the product is and be able to identify with it; and (c) you ought to use both audio and visual images. Other than those restrictions, you are free to try any new form.

The News Show

News shows are quite interesting to produce. Not only do you get the chance to work with television but also the chance to learn important news first and first hand.

Determine Your Coverage Area

The first step in planning a news program is to determine the coverage area for which you will be responsible. For example, will your news program be responsible just for school related news? Perhaps you would like to enlarge its responsibility to cover other activities of the students, perhaps teachers, perhaps administrators. You might also make it very large and include happenings in the community related to your audience. In determining the coverage area, remember that a news program dedicates itself to bringing all the news of importance from its coverage area to its audience. The audience has to be able to depend on the program for complete coverage of an area. Consequently, do not make the area larger than you can actually cover.

Determine the Format of the Program

News programs are put together by segments. A typical news program might have a section on "hard news" (the events of the day), one on sports, another on the weather, and finally, a commentary or editorial using someone's opinions or thoughts on a subject. The segments that are used and the amount of time given to each determines the format of the program. Usually, a different person is given responsibility for each segment within the format. It, then, becomes his or her responsibility to find the stories that will fill the time allocated.

Finding the Stories

Stories are the script of the news program. Getting a good story takes work. A story is usually many sided. More than one person or group is usually affected, and what might be good for one might not be so good for another. Check all the angles. If you have decided to put on a news show, everyone in the class should be involved in finding the stories. These ideas and tips should be funneled into a News Director. The News Director will assign a reporter to cover the story. The reporter will get the information and write the copy to be used on the program. The reporter has to check his facts, making sure they are correct, and to search out the story behind the story. Once all the stories are in for the day, it is the News Director's job to (a) select the ones that will be used on the program; (b) determine the order in which they will appear; and (c) edit them to fit the time allowed and to provide continuity between them.

The Perfect News Show

The perfect news show has yet to appear. Each format has its limitations; there never seems to be enough time; sometimes a big story will slip by. However, news has the satisfaction of bringing people what they need to know.

The Documentary Program

The documentary is a program that attempts to inform the audience about some subject of importance. It differs from news programs in that it is longer and usually explores the feelings behind the facts.

How To Select A Topic

The subject of a documentary can be a person, an event that has occured or is about to occur, and/or an issue of controversy. The subject should be of interest to your audience, and it will be if some value can be shown. Topics that have readily available information sources are to be preferred. Is there material in the library on the subject? Can the persons involved be interviewed? Will the story lend itself to visual images? These are useful questions to ask in selecting a topic.

The Issue of Objectivity

A good documentary tries to put together all the facts and opinions about the issue involved. It leaves the conclusions up to the viewers. The documentary is not an editorial. It does not espouse some action or solution. Actions may be proposed and evidence presented in their behalf, but they must be balanced by other perspectives.

The Content

Photographs, drawings and other art work, maps, interviews with the actual people, re-creation of interviews, dramatic re-creations, discussion panels, debates, on-the-spot film or tape coverage, magazines and newspapers, voice-over commentary, musical background and foreground, and even lectures can all be the content of your documentary.

The Entertainment Program

Most entertainment programs require camera and sound facilities beyond the one camera and one microphone equipment that we have been assuming. Of course, if you are lucky enough to be in a school with access to studio facilities, then you can produce almost anything. For most of us, the variety show and the media show will be our best bets in entertainment.

The Variety Show

In-school productions can easily handle variety shows composed of an Emcee and solo or small groups of performers. You will be surprised at the talent hiding in your classroom and in your school. Remember, a variety show depends on good coordination and a lively pace. Planning and rehearsal are absolutely necessary. Plan to spend several hours in rehearsal to make it right.

The Media Show

Not every entertainment program has to tell a story. A collection of photographs and/or art work with music or commentary can produce a very pleasant program. You can have fun with shots of familiar objects taken from odd angles or from very close or far away. Abstract shapes, swirling liquids, patterns of light and dark, a flower, an insect, a frog can all hold our interest for some period of time. Take a chance and experiment. Find out what you can say with television.

Chapter 9

STUDYING PERSONAL USES
OF TELEVISION

THE material that is included in this chapter was originally prepared for the use of older elementary and secondary school students. It was designed to guide and assist students in the careful study of their personal uses of television. Of course, in many situations, the parents and teachers of the students who were involved in pilot programs of critical viewing skills have kept diaries of their viewing and participated whole-heartedly in the study of personal uses of television. This adds to the value of the experience for the student.

Social studies and language arts skills are developed through the activity that requires students to collect information in a systematic manner, to organize and analyze this information, and finally, to write their own accounts of their uses of television.

For many students, and perhaps for many teachers, the study of themselves and the writing of an account based upon such data will be a first. Students are typically highly motivated at the outset of this activity, but the prospect of teachers and parents making negative judgments about a student's findings will surely diminish the enthusiasm for the undertaking.

It is important that teachers assure the students that the purpose of the self-study is to help them sharpen their inquiry skills, apply expository writing skills, and finally, evaluate the meaning their findings hold for them. As in so many other life situations, if people are to be "rewarded" for reporting false information, we should not be shocked at the absence of truth.

Beginning with the section on Data Collection, the material is presented just as it was written for use by teachers and students in classes where critical viewing skills were being taught. Although teachers usually make certain modifications to fit individual student and group needs, these materials and procedures have been found to be appropriate for use just as they appear here.

Basic skills that are attended to include the following:

1. Following written directions.
2. Recording information from primary sources.
3. Classifying information.
4. Summarizing information.
5. Evaluating information.
6. Organizing information for written reporting.
7. Reportorial writing.

As is the case with any learning activity, teachers will want to adapt procedures to fit student levels of readiness. We have found that students in middle elementary grades can handle the diary activity quite well. However, the analysis of the Apple-A-Day instrument using the Dimension Scores is recommended for older students only. For elementary students, it is sufficient that they tabulate and total each dimension of three items. This will enable them to discern that the reasons they watch one program may differ from the reasons for watching another.

Inasmuch as television programs come and go with each season, or sooner, it is a good idea to have the students update the examples provided for categories of television shows. This is, also, a good exercise in identification of programs by type, and classification with others of similar type.

The Student Questionnaire is useful, particularly with elementary age students, in building interest and personal involvement in the diary activity. It is suggested that you inform parents about the diary activity and its objectives since it is important that they realize that the school is neither snoopy nor is it promoting additional television watching. Parental support is essential.

DATA COLLECTION

You have studied many subjects during your years in school. Mathematics, science, history, all of these subjects have received a great deal of your time. Now, you are going to have a chance to study something about yourself, not everything about yourself but some of the things about you and the way you use television. Each of

STUDENT QUESTIONNAIRE

1. Write down the names of the three television programs that you watch more often than any other program.

	Name of Program	Time of Day	Circle Day of Week
a.	_____	_____	S M T W Th F Sa
b.	_____	_____	S M T W Th F Sa
c.	_____	_____	S M T W Th F Sa

2. What reasons can you give for liking the programs that you watch?

	Program	Why You Like It
a.	_____	_____
b.	_____	_____
c.	_____	_____

3. Have you watched any of your three favorites for as long as (circle one)

   1 year?   2 years?   5 years?

4. How many hours each week do you think you spend watching television?

   _____5 hours or less   _____15 to 20 hours

   _____5 to 10 hours   _____more than 20 hours

   _____10 to 15 hours

5. Is TV watching your favorite past time? _____yes _____no

6. What do you like to do that is more fun than watching TV? _____

   _____

7. Do you think you watch too much TV? _____yes _____no

8. Why do you watch TV?

   _____Programs are fun to watch   _____Nothing else to do

   _____Because family are watching   _____Keep from doing something I
                                                     don't want to do

Figure 3. Student Questionnaire.

us uses television in a special way that is different from anyone else's use. We have prepared this section to help you study yourself and television.

Most of the time you have studied a subject by using books that already had all the information you needed. This topic — you and television — has no textbook because only you can write it. Consequently, we planned some activities to help you get the information you need about yourself. The first section of the activity deals with *fact collection*. The second section will help you understand these facts through *fact analysis*. The third section will privide the *story about you*. You can see that these are common sense activities. You obtain information, figure out what it means, and then tell about it in a summary of the facts.

The first activity gives us a way to record our television watching behavior over a period of time so that we can gather information about our television watching habits. The methods we will be using are the same methods that scientists use when they study people's television viewing habits. So, each of us will work like a scientist while we carefully record the facts of our television viewing. When scientists collect facts, they call those facts data (a single fact would be a datum). The data that we will be collecting and analyzing will tell us a great deal about ourselves.

The Diary

The data we want to collect will describe our televiewing habits. The instrument we will use to collect these data is called a "Diary of Television Viewing." The complete diary is shown in Figure 6 as a model for your use. The diary calls for you to record each television program you watched for at least ten minutes. Then, you will note any "activity trade-offs" and the types of programs you watched. Part of one page of the diary is reproduced so that we can take a close look at it. We took Figure 4 from the diary of a friend to show you what a completed page would look like. She started watching television at 6:00 in the evening. She watched only eleven minutes of *Star Trek*. She did not want to be doing anything else, but she should have (actually, she should have been setting the table which she finally went to do). At 7:00 she turned the television on again to watch *Wild Kingdom*. She was content to sit and did not have anything else to do. At 7:30 she watched a game show, *Let's Make A Deal*. She wanted to be doing something else, but she did not have to. At 8:00 she apparently found something else to do for she stopped viewing then.

It is pretty surprising how much we know about her just from her three lines of data. You will be surprised, too, about how much you can learn about yourself when you complete the diary.

This section records the time that you watched the program.	Name of the program watched for ten minutes or more (only one per line, please)	If you had the chance is there something else you'd rather be doing?		If you're putting off something by watching TV, check yes here.	
Time		Rather Be Doing Something Else		Should Be Doing Something Else	
From To	Name of Program	Yes	No	Yes	No
6:00-6:11	Star Trek		✓	✓	
7:00-7:30	Wild Kingdom		✓		✓
7:30-8:00	Let's Make A Deal	✓			✓
Total # of Checks In Each Column		1	2	1	2
		Yes	No	Yes	No

Figure 4. Sample Diary Form, portion completed.

The diary is set up so you can record your viewing beginning on a Saturday and running from that Saturday through the following weekend. That will give you two Saturdays, two Sundays, and five weekdays during which you can record your viewing. There is one diary page for each day of the survey period. Make an entry for each program that you watch for at least ten minutes. Each entry should account for at least ten minutes of viewing but not more than thirty minutes of viewing. If a program runs more than thirty minutes, make a new entry after each thirty minutes of viewing. For example, if you watched *Wide World of Sports* for an hour and fifteen minutes, your entries might look like Figure 5. If you examine the entries, you can see why more than one entry is needed. Our person in the example changed as she watched. She decided she wanted to be doing something else. A single entry would not have recorded this change. Those changes are an important part of the analysis section. Consequently, make an entry for each half hour of viewing.

The Apple-A-Day Questionnaire

On the back of each diary page is the beginning of another

Time		Name of Program	Rather Be Doing Something Else		Should Be Doing Something Else	
From	To		Yes	No	Yes	No
3:00-3:30		Wide World of Sports		✓		✓
3:30-4:00		"	✓			✓
4:00-4:15		"	✓			✓

Figure 5. Sample Diary Form, portion completed.

measurement instrument. We have called it the "Apple-A-Day" measurement instrument (Figure 7) because you fill it out once each day of the survey period. The Apple-A-Day instrument gathers information about the reasons we watch the programs we watch. The instrument first asks you to select a television program you have watched. It could be one you watched that day or one that you have seen some other time.

Once you have selected your program and written the name in the space provided, the instrument presents twenty-seven sentences, each one a reason why you might watch the program. All you have to do is read each statement to see if it gives a reason why you watch the program you selected. For example, you watch a program on Friday night because you rarely have anything else to do on that night. You come to the statement:

I watch this program because I have nothing else to do.
Strongly Agree   Agree   Neutral   Disagree Strongly   Disagree

Well, yes, this statement expresses at least one of the reasons why you watch this program. Consequently, you would agree with it. Since, in this case, it describes the main reason you watch, you would strongly agree with it and would circle the *strongly agree* answer. You would go through the other twenty-six statements in the same way. You would agree with those that seemed to be a reason you have watched the program. You would disagree with those statements that rarely describe why you watch. If you were not sure about a statement, you would circle the *neutral* response.

Filling out the Apple-A-Day instrument will let you find out about your reasons for watching programs. Later, when your class is together, you will be able to see why other people watch the programs you do. It is always interesting to see the many different reasons people watch the same program.

Scientific work requires a good deal of care. If we are careless about our data collection, then we will be wrong in our analysis. (Scientists call this the GIGO effect — *Garbage In, Garbage Out*). Remember, the information you are collecting is about yourself and nobody deserves a better job than you. Fill out your diary while you watch television. Memory can play tricks on us if we wait until the next day. Complete the Apple-A-Day instrument each day, making sure each statement has a response. You are a fascinating person; find out about you.

Diary Form

DAY OF THE WEEK _____

Time		Name of Program	Rather Be Doing Something Else		Should Be Doing Something Else		Type of Program
From	To		Yes	No	Yes	No	
Total # of Checks In Each Column							
			Yes	No	Yes	No	

Figure 6. Diary Form.

THE "APPLE-A-DAY" MEASUREMENT INSTRUMENT

Please complete this questionnaire once each day during the survey week. People watch television for different reasons at different times. Sometimes they watch to find out what is going on. Sometimes they watch to be entertained. Select one program that you've watched today. Then, read each of the following statements and figure out whether you agree or disagree with the statement. Mark the statement according to the degree that you do agree or disagree. For example, if you like very much to watch your program because it brings people into your home, then you would agree strongly with the statement and you would check the agree strongly position. Please go on now and mark each statement according to the degree that you agree or disagree.

NAME OF PROGRAM_____

1. I watch this program because when I watch I can be like the people on the show.

    Agree Strongly   Agree   Neutral   Disagree   Disagree Strongly

2. I watch this program because it helps me answer questions about how people act in different social situations.

    Agree Strongly   Agree   Neutral   Disagree   Disagree Strongly

3. I watch this program because it gives me and my family or friends something to do when we're together.

    Agree Strongly   Agree   Neutral   Disagree   Disagree Strongly

4. I watch this program because it eases the pressures of the day.

    Agree Strongly   Agree   Neutral   Disagree   Disagree Strongly

5. I watch this program because it helps me realize what I've got in comparison with what other people have.

    Agree Strongly   Agree   Neutral   Disagree   Disagree Strongly

6. I watch this program because it brings people into my home.

    Agree Strongly   Agree   Neutral   Disagree   Disagree Strongly

7. I watch this program because it keeps me on the edge of my chair.

    Agree Strongly   Agree   Neutral   Disagree   Disagree Strongly

8. I watch this program because it cheers me up.

    Agree Strongly   Agree   Neutral   Disagree   Disagree Strongly

Figure 7. The "Apple-A-Day" Measurement Instrument.

9. I watch this program because it just happens to be on.

    Agree Strongly   Agree   Neutral   Disagree   Disagree Strongly

10. I watch this program because it shows me people I'd like to be like.

    Agree Strongly   Agree   Neutral   Disagree   Disagree Strongly

11. I watch this program because it shows me what to do when someone is with other people.

    Agree Strongly   Agree   Neutral   Disagree   Disagree Strongly

12. I watch this program because it gives me a chance to get together with my family or friends.

    Agree Strongly   Agree   Neutral   Disagree   Disagree Strongly

13. I watch this program because I can get my mind off my own problems.

    Agree Strongly   Agree   Neutral   Disagree   Disagree Strongly

14. I watch this program because it lets me compare my life with other people's lives.

    Agree Strongly   Agree   Neutral   Disagree   Disagree Strongly

15. I watch this program because I get interested in the people on the show.

    Agree Strongly   Agree   Neutral   Disagree   Disagree Strongly

16. I watch this program because of the physical action in it.

    Agree Strongly   Agree   Neutral   Disagree   Disagree Strongly

17. I watch this program because it gives me a chance to laugh.

    Agree Strongly   Agree   Neutral   Disagree   Disagree Strongly

18. I watch this program because its not as bad as the rest.

    Agree Strongly   Agree   Neutral   Disagree   Disagree Strongly

19. I watch this program because I can believe that I'm like the characters on the show.

    Agree Strongly   Agree   Neutral   Disagree   Disagree Strongly

20. I watch this program because I can learn how people should act with other people.

    Agree Strongly   Agree   Neutral   Disagree   Disagree Strongly

Figure 7 *continued.*

21. I watch this program because I can watch with my family or friends.

Agree Strongly   Agree   Neutral   Disagree   Disagree Strongly

22. I watch this program because it is an entertaining way to forget my cares.

Agree Strongly   Agree   Neutral   Disagree   Disagree Strongly

23. I watch this program because I can see what I'm getting out of life and what other people are getting out of life.

Agree Strongly   Agree   Neutral   Disagree   Disagree Strongly

24. I watch this program because the people on it seem like they're talking to me.

Agree Strongly   Agree   Neutral   Disagree   Disagree Strongly

25. I watch this program because some of the characters are exciting.

Agree Strongly   Agree   Neutral   Disagree   Disagree Strongly

26. I watch this program because it brightens my day.

Agree Strongly   Agree   Neutral   Disagree   Disagree Strongly

27. I watch this program because there is nothing better on.

Agree Strongly   Agree   Neutral   Disagree   Disagree Strongly

Figure 7 *continued.*

DATA ANALYSIS

You have now collected information about yourself using two data collection instruments, The Diary and the Apple-A-Day questionnaire. Now is the time to take a careful look at the information you have collected to figure out what it means.

First Half — The Diary

First, take a look at The Diary. The diary collects four separate pieces of information: (1) the time that you watch; (2) the programs that you watch; (3) the activity trade-offs that might be occurring, and (4) types of programs you watched.

Part I — The Time That You Watch

When we analyze data, the major thing we look for are patterns. Patterns in the data tip us off to consistent behaviors, which in turn suggest that we have ideas, values, or attitudes in our mind about

FORM A

WHEN DO YOU WATCH?

WEEKDAY VIEWING

Daytime	M	T	W	T	F	Total # of Boxes	Evening	M	T	W	T	F	Total # of Boxes
6:00 - 6:14							4:00 - 4:14						
6:15 - 6:29							4:15 - 4:29						
6:30 - 6:44							4:30 - 4:44						
6:45 - 6:59							4:45 - 4:59						
7:00 - 7:14							5:00 - 5:14						
7:15 - 7:29							5:15 - 5:29						
7:30 - 7:44							5:30 - 5:44						
7:45 - 7:59							5:45 - 5:59						
8:00 - 8:14							6:00 - 6:14						
8:15 - 8:29							6:15 - 6:29						
8:30 - 8:44							6:30 - 6:44						
8:45 - 8:59							6:45 - 6:59						
9:00 - 9:14							7:00 - 7:14						
9:15 - 9:29							7:15 - 7:29						
9:30 - 9:44							7:30 - 7:44						
9:45 - 9:59							7:45 - 7:59						
10:00 - 10:14							8:00 - 8:14						
10:15 - 10:29							8:15 - 8:29						
10:30 - 10:44							8:30 - 8:44						
10:45 - 10:59							8:45 - 8:59						
11:00 - 11:14							9:00 - 9:14						
11:15 - 11:29							9:15 - 9:29						
11:30 - 11:44							9:30 - 9:44						
11:45 - 11:59							9:45 - 9:59						
Noon - 12:14							10:00 - 10:14						
12:15 - 12:29							10:15 - 10:29						
12:30 - 12:44							10:30 - 10:44						
12:45 - 12:59							10:45 - 10:59						
1:00 - 1:14							11:00 - 11:14						
1:15 - 1:29							11:15 - 11:29						
1:30 - 1:44							11:30 - 11:44						
1:45 - 1:59							11:45 - 11:59						
2:00 - 2:14							Mid. - 12:14						
2:15 - 2:29							12:15 - 12:29						
2:30 - 2:44							12:30 - 12:44						
2:45 - 2:59							12:45 - 12:59						
3:00 - 3:14							1:00 - 1:14						
3:15 - 3:29							1:15 - 1:29						
3:30 - 3:44							1:30 - 1:44						
3:45 - 3:59							1:45 - 1:59						
Total = of Boxes							Total = of Boxes						

Figure 8. Form A.

how things are. The first analysis procedure, then, lets us look for patterns in the times that we watch television. This handbook provides you with two forms to analyze the time data, one for weekday viewing and one for weekend viewing.

Form A (Figure 8), which is for weekday viewing, is very simple to complete. The form has each quarter hour (15 minutes) from 6:00 in the morning until 2:00 A.M. that night for each weekday (Monday, Tuesday, Wednesday, Thursday, and Friday). All you have to do is to put a check mark in each quarter hour where you watched some television according to what you recorded in your diary. Consequently, you would start by taking your diary sheet for Monday. Then, you would check off all the times you watched on that Monday. If you started that Monday by watching a morning show from 7:00 to 7:30 before going off to school, you would therefore, put a check in the quarter hour marked 7:00-7:14 and the one marked 7:15-7:29. How about 7:30-7:44? We said we viewed from 7:00-7:30. We would leave that one blank. Half hour television shows do not actually run thirty minutes; they run just a few seconds less than thirty minutes. If you watch a few minutes of the next show — the one that started at 7:30 — then, you would put a check in the 7:30-7:44 box. Note that you record any viewing during any quarter hour even if it is just for a few minutes during that period.

Putting a check in all those quarter hour boxes takes time, and it is easy to make a mistake. We would suggest using a pencil to make your check marks. It is probably a good idea to spread the work out over a couple of days.

Form B (Figure 9) is just like Form A except that it is for weekend viewing. Since Saturday is a special program day, we have separated the two diary Saturdays from the two diary Sundays. Saturday[1] means the first Saturday on the survey period; Saturday[2] means the second Saturday.

Part II — The Programs That You Watch

The next analytical task is to determine the kind of programs that you watch. Form C (Figure 10) presents seventeen categories of television programs. Examples of programs that fit each category are given. Your job is to sort each program that you watched into one of the program categories. Sorting the programs that you watched into these categories will allow you to discover the kinds of programs you like best.

FORM B

WHEN DO YOU WATCH?

WEEKEND VIEWING

Daytime	Sat.¹	Sat.²	Total # of Boxes	Sun.¹	Sun.²	Total # of Boxes	Evening	Sat.¹	Sat.²	Total # of Boxes	Sun.¹	Sun.²	Total #
6:00 - 6:14							4:00 - 4:14						
6:15 - 6:29							4:15 - 4:29						
6:30 - 6:44							4:30 - 4:44						
6:45 - 6:59							4:45 - 4:59						
7:00 - 7:14							5:00 - 5:14						
7:15 - 7:29							5:15 - 5:29						
7:30 - 7:44							5:30 - 5:44						
7:45 - 7:59							5:45 - 5:59						
8:00 - 8:14							6:00 - 6:14						
8:15 - 8:29							6:15 - 6:29						
8:30 - 8:44							6:30 - 6:44						
8:45 - 8:59							6:45 - 6:59						
9:00 - 9:14							7:00 - 7:14						
9:15 - 9:29							7:15 - 7:29						
9:30 - 9:44							7:30 - 7:44						
9:45 - 9:59							7:45 - 7:59						
10:00 - 10:14							8:00 - 8:14						
10:15 - 10:29							8:15 - 8:29						
10:30 - 10:44							8:30 - 8:44						
10:45 - 10:59							8:45 - 8:59						
11:00 - 11:14							9:00 - 9:14						
11:15 - 11:29							9:15 - 9:29						
11:30 - 11:44							9:30 - 9:44						
11:45 - 11:59							9:45 - 9:59						
Noon - 12:14							10:00 - 10:14						
12:15 - 12:29							10:15 - 10:29						
12:30 - 12:44							10:30 - 10:44						
12:45 - 12:59							10:45 - 10:59						
1:00 - 1:14							11:00 - 11:14						
1:15 - 1:29							11:15 - 11:29						
1:30 - 1:44							11:30 - 11:44						
1:45 - 1:59							11:45 - 11:59						
2:00 - 2:14							Mid. - 12:14						
2:15 - 2:29							12:15 - 12:29						
2:30 - 2:44							12:30 - 12:44						
2:45 - 2:59							12:45 - 12:59						
3:00 - 3:14							1:00 - 1:14						
3:15 - 3:29							1:15 - 1:29						
3:30 - 3:44							1:30 - 1:44						
3:45 - 3:59							1:45 - 1:59						
Total = of Boxes							Total = of Boxes						

Figure 9. Form B.

Part III — Analysis of the "Should Be's" and the "Rather Be's"

Form D (Figure 11) asks you to record the number of yeses and the number of noes for the "rather be" and the "should be" questions for each day of the survey period. Since you have already counted and recorded those numbers on the diary page, all you have to do is to transfer those figures to this form.

FORM C

Category	Tallies--Put one mark for each program of a given type watched	Total # of Tallies this row
Action Adventure		
Situation Comedy		
Situation Drama		
Comedy Variety		
Game Shows		
Special Target Shows		
Cartoon Situation Comedy		
Cartoon Action Adventure		
Cartoon Action Comedy		
Sports		
Soaps		
Westerns		
Outdoors		
Contemporary Music		
Talk		
News		
News Magazine		

Figure 10. Form C.

EXPLANATION OF FORM C

Categories for Television Shows With Sample Programs

AA   *Action/Adventure/Police/Private Detective*
         Chips; Dukes of Hazzard; Quincy; Hart to Hart; Hill Street

Blues; Nero Wolfe

SC   *Situation Comedy*
Archie Bunker's Place; Benson; I'm A Big Girl Now; One Day at a Time; Happy Days; Three's Company

SD   *Situation Drama*
Little House on the Prairie; The Waltons; Eight is Enough; Lou Grant; M*A*S*H

CV   *Comedy Variety*
Carol Burnett and Friends; Muppet Show; Hee Haw

GS   *Game Shows*
Name that Tune; Hollywood Squares; Joker's Wild; Family Feud; Jeopardy; Tic Tac Dough; Let's Make a Deal

SP   *Sports*
Football; Basketball; Golf; Baseball

S   *Soaps*
Search for Tomorrow; General Hospital; Dallas; Another World; All My Children; Young and Restless

W   *Westerns*
Wild Wild West; Kung Fu

O   *Outdoors*
Jimmy Houston Outdoors; Wild Kingdom; Jacques Costeau; Last of the Wild

CM   *Contemporary Music*
Country Top 20; Country Classic; American Bandstand; Soul Train; Midnight Special

T   *Talk*
The Tonight Show; Phil Donahue; John Davidson; Dick Cavett

N   *News*
All news programs, network and local

NM   *News Magazine*
Issues and Answers; MacNeil Lehrer; Firing Line; Bill Moyers Journal; 60 Minutes; Black Perspective

STS   *Special Target Shows*
Over Easy; Big Blue Marble; 3-2-1 Contact; Disney's Won-

derful World; Zoom

CSC *Cartoon Situation Comedy*
Fat Albert; Jetsons; Fonz; Flintstones; My Favorite Martian

CAA *Cartoon Action Adventure*
Superfriends; Johnny Quest; Tarzan/Lone Ranger; Drak Pack; Thundarr

CAC *Cartoon Action Comedy*
Tom and Jerry; Bugs Bunny; Scooby and Scrappy Do; Hong Kong Phooey

FORM D

Day of Week	Rather Be Question		Should Be Question	
	Yes	No	Yes	No
Monday				
Tuesday				
Wednesday				
Thursday				
Friday				
Saturday[1]				
Saturday[2]				
Sunday[1]				
Sunday[2]				
Total for Each Column				
	Total Yesses	Total Noes	Total Yesses	Total Noes

Figure 11. Form D

Second Half — The Apple-A-Day Instrument

You will remember that the Apple-A-Day instrument was made up of twenty-seven statements. Those twenty-seven statements represent nine different reasons for watching television. Each reason has three statements or sentences that make up a part of it. Scientists sometimes call these reasons dimensions or factors. Our last form, Form E (Figure 12) shows you which statements make up each reason. We have not given names to the factors or reasons as we

FORM E

NAME OF PROGRAM _____

TYPE OF PROGRAM _____

Item		Score 1=SA 2=A 3=N 4=E 5=SD	Dimension Score Total Divided by 3	If Total Is	Then Dimension Score Is
1	I can be like the people on the show			3	1.00
10	People I'd like to be like			4	1.33
19	I'm like the characters on the show			5	1.66
	TOTAL			6	2.00
2	People act in different social situations			7	2.33
11	What to do when someone is with other people			8	2.66
20	Should act with other people			9	3.00
	TOTAL			10	3.33
3	Something to do when we're together			11	3.66
12	Get together with my family or friends			12	4.00
21	Watch with my family or friends			13	4.33
	TOTAL			14	4.66
4	It eases the pressures of the day			15	5.00
13	My mind off my own problems				
22	Way to forget my cares				
	TOTAL				
5	Helps me realize what I've got				
14	Compare my life				
23	Getting out of life				
	TOTAL				

Figure 12. Form E.

FORM E-continued

Item		S 1 =SA 2 =A 3 =N 4 =D 5 =SD	Dimension Score Total Divided by 3
6	It brings people into my home		/
15	I get interested in the poeple		/
24	They're talking to me		/
	TOTAL		
7	Keeps me on the edge of my chair		/
16	Physical action in it		/
25	Some of the characters are exciting		/
	TOTAL		
8	It cheers me up		/
17	Gives me a chance to laugh		/
26	Brightens my day		/
	TOTAL		
9	Just happens to be on		/
18	Not as bad as the rest		/
27	Nothing better on		/
	TOTAL		

Figure 12 *continued.*

thought you might like to do that. Perhaps, you would call the first one "Make Believe," "Identification," or whatever is your idea of the best name.

The way you use Form E might look a little complicated and it is. However, you have made it through before. First, you complete one Form E for each day you rated. You rated one program per day for nine days, consequently, that means nine Forms of E.

The form presents a shortened version of each statement (the whole sentence would not fit). The statements are presented in a new order. Notice that the first section asks you to score statements 1, 10, and 19; the second calls for 2, 11, and 20; and so on. The statements were mixed up on the Apple-A-Day instrument so we could hide the dimensions. (Why would that be a good idea?)

Score each statement by giving it a 1 if you strongly agreed; a 2 if you agreed; a 3 if you were neutral; a 4 if you disagreed; a 5 if you strongly disagreed.

After you have scored each statement, you can calculate the dimension score. The dimension score is the average of the three statement scores. To get an average of a set of numbers, add the number and divide by the number of numbers. Each dimension has three statements. Consequently, we would add the three scores from the statements together and then divide that total by the number of numbers we added (which was three if we did it right). To save you some work, we have given you a handy guide for dividing the total by three (aren't we nice?).

Note that at the top of Form E are blanks for the name of the program and for the type of program. Get the type of program from the list of program categories you used in completing Form C. The name and type of program will be useful in case you want to compare with someone else the reasons you watch a particular program or program type.

Analyzing data is exciting and interesting, but it also can be tedious and frustrating. It is fascinating to search out patterns in the data and to begin to make sense of all the information you collected. It is also hard work and easy to make mistakes and to get discouraged. Do not try to do all your analyses in one day. Give yourself some time. When you get tired, take a break. The data will always be there waiting for you to unlock the story that they hold.

CASE STUDY NARRATIVES — THE STORY ABOUT YOU

We have done a lot of work in those other sections to get to this point, but it is worth it, for now we will be able to write the story of the way we use television — or at least, a good part of that story. The data themselves tell us *what* we do with television. This part of the task will get to the question of *why*. The answers to questions of why-we-do-things are not readily at hand. All of us have been asked why we did something, only to answer "I don't know" — usually with our head hung low. To answer the question of why we watch television when we do and why we watch the programs we watch, we will have to use our memory and our data to recreate the situation.

FORM A

WHEN DO YOU WATCH?

WEEKDAY VIEWING

Daytime	M	T	W	T	F	Total # of Boxes	Evening	M	T	W	T	F	Total # of Boxes
6:00 - 6:14							4:00 - 4:14						
6:15 - 6:29							4:15 - 4:29						
6:30 - 6:44							4:30 - 4:44						
6:45 - 6:59							4:45 - 4:59						
7:00 - 7:14				X		1	5:00 - 5:14						
7:15 - 7:29				X		1	5:15 - 5:29						
7:30 - 7:44							5:30 - 5:44						
7:45 - 7:59							5:45 - 5:59						
8:00 - 8:14							6:00 - 6:14						
8:15 - 8:29							6:15 - 6:29						
8:30 - 8:44							6:30 - 6:44						
8:45 - 8:59							6:45 - 6:59						
9:00 - 9:14							7:00 - 7:14						
9:15 - 9:29							7:15 - 7:29						
9:30 - 9:44							7:30 - 7:44						
9:45 - 9:59							7:45 - 7:59						
10:00 - 10:14							8:00 - 8:14	X					1
10:15 - 10:29							8:15 - 8:29	X					1
10:30 - 10:44							8:30 - 8:44			X			1
10:45 - 10:59							8:45 - 8:59			X			1
11:00 - 11:14							9:00 - 9:14		X			X	2
11:15 - 11:29							9:15 - 9:29		X			X	2
11:30 - 11:44							9:30 - 9:44					X	1
11:45 - 11:59							9:45 - 9:59					X	1
Noon - 12:14							10:00 - 10:14						
12:15 - 12:29							10:15 - 10:29						
12:30 - 12:44							10:30 - 10:44	X					1
12:45 - 12:59							10:45 - 10:59	X					1
1:00 - 1:14							11:00 - 11:14						
1:15 - 1:29							11:15 - 11:29						
1:30 - 1:44							11:30 - 11:44						
1:45 - 1:59							11:45 - 11:59						
2:00 - 2:14							Mid. - 12:14						
2:15 - 2:29							12:15 - 12:29						
2:30 - 2:44							12:30 - 12:44						
2:45 - 2:59							12:45 - 12:59						
3:00 - 3:14	X					1	1:00 - 1:14						
3:15 - 3:29	X					1	1:15 - 1:29						
3:30 - 3:44	X					1	1:30 - 1:44						
3:45 - 3:59	X					1	1:45 - 1:59						
Total = of Boxes	4			2			Total = of Boxes	4	2	2			

Figure 13. Sample of Form A completed.

We will take each of the forms in turn and see what kind of story we can tell.

Part I — The Times That We Watch

This part deals with forms A and B. Assume that there are two times when we watch television: (1) when there is a program (or programs) that is of specific interest to us; and (2) when what we want to do is "watch television" and the program that we select is of lesser interest. Scientists call these decisions content-related in the first case and content-free in the second. These two decisions usually result in different patterns of viewing showing up on the time forms. Content-related viewing will show different patterns for each day.

FORM A

WHEN DO YOU WATCH?

WEEKDAY VIEWING

Daytime	M	T	W	T	F	Total # of Boxes	Evening	M	T	W	T	F	Total # of Boxes
6:00 - 6:14							4:00 - 4:14						
6:15 - 6:29							4:15 - 4:29						
6:30 - 6:44							4:30 - 4:44						
6:45 - 6:59							4:45 - 4:59						
7:00 - 7:14							5:00 - 5:14						
7:15 - 7:29							5:15 - 5:29						
7:30 - 7:44							5:30 - 5:44						
7:45 - 7:59							5:45 - 5:59						
8:00 - 8:14							6:00 - 6:14						
8:15 - 8:29							6:15 - 6:29						
8:30 - 8:44							6:30 - 6:44						
8:45 - 8:59							6:45 - 6:59						
9:00 - 9:14							7:00 - 7:14						
9:15 - 9:29							7:15 - 7:29						
9:30 - 9:44							7:30 - 7:44						
9:45 - 9:59							7:45 - 7:59						
10:00 - 10:14							8:00 - 8:14	X	X	X	X	X	5
10:15 - 10:29							8:15 - 8:29	X	X	X	X	X	5
10:30 - 10:44							8:30 - 8:44	X	X	X	X	X	5
10:45 - 10:59							8:45 - 8:59	X	X	X	X	X	5
11:00 - 11:14							9:00 - 9:14	X	X	X	X	X	5
11:15 - 11:29							9:15 - 9:29	X	X	X	X	X	5
11:30 - 11:44							9:30 - 9:44	X	X	X	X	X	5
11:45 - 11:59							9:45 - 9:59	X	X	X	X	X	5
Noon - 12:14							10:00 - 10:14						
12:15 - 12:29							10:15 - 10:29						
12:30 - 12:44							10:30 - 10:44						
12:45 - 12:59							10:45 - 10:59						
1:00 - 1:14							11:00 - 11:14						
1:15 - 1:29							11:15 - 11:29						
1:30 - 1:44							11:30 - 11:44						
1:45 - 1:59							11:45 - 11:59						
2:00 - 2:14							Mid. - 12:14						
2:15 - 2:29							12:15 - 12:29						
2:30 - 2:44							12:30 - 12:44						
2:45 - 2:59							12:45 - 12:59						
3:00 - 3:14							1:00 - 1:14						
3:15 - 3:29	X	X	X	X	X	5	1:15 - 1:29						
3:30 - 3:44	X	X	X	X	X	5	1:30 - 1:44						
3:45 - 3:59	X	X	X	X	X	5	1:45 - 1:59						
Total = of Boxes	3	3	3	3	3		Total = of Boxes	8	8	8	8	8	

Figure 14. Sample of Form A completed.

Content-free viewing will usually show up as a repeated pattern across days.

A person who makes all of his decisions to watch on a content-related basis might have a pattern of viewing times like Figure 13. Content-related decisions usually show up as isolated occurrences with little pattern of repetition across days.

Content-related decisions can be described as those decisions where the viewer has gone to the television listings in the newspaper or turned to his television magazine and found specific programs he considers of interest. Content-related decisions usually are not those where a person eases himself down in front of the set, flips it on, and settles back to watch what is there. That person is there to watch *television*, not a specific program.

A person who watches television and not programs would tend to present viewing patterns like Figure 14. Note that the person views in regular time blocks: always right after school and always from 8:00 to 10:00 P.M. each night. This person would watch during this time regardless of what programs were on.

Most of us make a mixed bag of decisions, that is, some of them are content-related and some of them are content-free. One such person's time form looked like Figure 15. We will take a close look at it and see if we can identify the content-free and content-related decisions. Starting at the top, the first thing we notice is that this person always watches one of the early morning shows. To find out why, the person would ask "What am I doing at that time which leads me to have the television on? Well, I'm always making and eating breakfast at that time. I guess I like to have the television on to keep track of the time and to keep me company."

Going down the form, we see that this person does not watch much television. He did watch his favorite show on Wednesday night. Then, he watched most of the evening on Friday. Why? "Oh, I was tired that night and did not want to do anything else. I watched to keep from getting bored."

From his thoughts and analysis, this person could write the following description about himself:

> I regularly use television in the morning to keep me company (and awake) and to keep track of the time.
> I do not watch television during the day because I am busy doing other things.

FORM A

WHEN DO YOU WATCH?

WEEKDAY VIEWING

Daytime	M	T	W	T	F	Total # of Boxes	Evening	M	T	W	T	F	Total # of Boxes
6:00 - 6:14							4:00 - 4:14						
6:15 - 6:29							4:15 - 4:29						
6:30 - 6:44							4:30 - 4:44						
6:45 - 6:59							4:45 - 4:59						
7:00 - 7:14							5:00 - 5:14						
7:15 - 7:29							5:15 - 5:29						
7:30 - 7:44							5:30 - 5:44						
7:45 - 7:59							5:45 - 5:59						
8:00 - 8:14							6:00 - 6:14						
8:15 - 8:29							6:15 - 6:29						
8:30 - 8:44							6:30 - 6:44						
8:45 - 8:59							6:45 - 6:59						
9:00 - 9:14	X	X	X	X	X	5	7:00 - 7:14						
9:15 - 9:29	X	X	X	X	X	5	7:15 - 7:29						
9:30 - 9:44	X	X	X	X	X	5	7:30 - 7:44						
9:45 - 9:59							7:45 - 7:59						
10:00 - 10:14							8:00 - 8:14			X		X	2
10:15 - 10:29							8:15 - 8:29			X		X	2
10:30 - 10:44							8:30 - 8:44			X		X	2
10:45 - 10:59							8:45 - 8:59			X		X	2
11:00 - 11:14							9:00 - 9:14					X	1
11:15 - 11:29							9:15 - 9:29					X	1
11:30 - 11:44							9:30 - 9:44					X	1
11:45 - 11:59							9:45 - 9:59					X	1
Noon - 12:14							10:00 - 10:14					X	1
12:15 - 12:29							10:15 - 10:29					X	1
12:30 - 12:44							10:30 - 10:44						
12:45 - 12:59							10:45 - 10:59						
1:00 - 1:14							11:00 - 11:14						
1:15 - 1:29							11:15 - 11:29						
1:30 - 1:44							11:30 - 11:44						
1:45 - 1:59							11:45 - 11:59						
2:00 - 2:14							Mid. - 12:14						
2:15 - 2:29							12:15 - 12:29						
2:30 - 2:44							12:30 - 12:44						
2:45 - 2:59							12:45 - 12:59						
3:00 - 3:14							1:00 - 1:14						
3:15 - 3:29							1:15 - 1:29						
3:30 - 3:44							1:30 - 1:44						
3:45 - 3:59							1:45 - 1:59						
Total # of Boxes	3	3	3	3	3		Total # of Boxes				4	10	

Figure 15. Sample of Form A completed.

In the evenings, I will watch if there is a program I really like. Sometimes, I watch television when I have nothing else to do.

Are you ready to write your own story? Start with Form A — your weekday viewing. Check first for content-free viewing. Regular patterns of viewing at the same time each day *usually* mean content-free viewing. When you find a regular pattern of viewing, ask yourself why you view at that time. Determine what happens in the time just before you watch and the time just after you finish. You might watch every night just before supper. The reason that you watch might be that it keeps you in the house ready to sit down the moment dinner is served. Of course, you might not do that at all, but that is the way to interrogate, question, analyze those regular patterns.

Sometimes regular patterns appear because other activities are not available. Ask yourself "What would I give up to watch television at that time?" If it would not take much to draw you away, then it suggests that watching television at that time is due more to the lack of other opportunities than the importance of television.

A regular pattern does not always mean content-free viewing. It might mean that the best shows are on at that time each night. One way to check for that is to ask yourself "Would I be upset if as the show was starting someone asked to change the channel to a program that person would prefer?" If you would be upset, then the program has, at least, some importance. Of course, there can be both content-free and content-related reasons for viewing at a particular time.

For each viewing block write a sentence in your story of why you are viewing at that time. Content-free viewing blocks can be described with the reasons why you think watching television occurs then — nothing else to do; to be ready for supper, etc. Content-related viewing can be described with the reasons you like the program — it is exciting or fun, etc. Viewing that has a combination of reasons can have both kinds of descriptions.

There are a couple of other things to look for in this form. The white spaces — when you do not view — are as important as the filled in ones. The explanation for many of them will be simple — you are in school or at work. Others might relate to the kinds of shows that are on or the importance you attach to activities other than watching television.

The day of the week may be important to the way you view. Friday night may be different from all other week nights. Saturday morning is a special television morning, so look for special patterns there.

A rule of thumb in all data snooping is to account for each unit of data. Our data here are the fifteen minute time periods. Your story should have something to say about all of them.

Part II — The Kinds of Shows You Most Often Watch

In this part, we will take a look at Form C. Form C, you will remember, had you sorting the programs out into seventeen categories or types. In our case study, we are going to use four of those program categories — the two you watch the most and the two you watch the least. Therefore, get out Form C and determine which two categories have the largest totals. If you find more than two — that is you have ties — pick the two you like the best. Once you have determined these two categories, think a bit to figure out what it is about these shows that you like. Is it the stories or the people or the action or what? After figuring out what you like about these kinds of shows, jot down a sentence or two explaining what you like about them. For example, you might say "My favorite type of programs have stars who can sing and tell jokes and my next favorite programs have stories that are exciting and somewhat scary.

Now find the two categories which you watch the least. First rule: Skip all those categories that have no tally marks at all. In this case, the lowest score is 1, not zero. If you have more than two low scoring categories, pick the two you *like the least*. Second rule: Do not include in this list categories of shows you really like, but just happened not to watch. For example, if you really like to watch sports but could watch only one program this week, do not include sports in this "do not like" list. When you are sure you have the two categories you like the least, write a sentence or two about each describing what you *do not like* about them. An example might be: "Shows I do not like are those with stories that are too simple; it is too easy to figure them out. The next type I do not like are talk shows where no one has anything interesting to say."

Part III — What the "Rather Be's" and "Should Be's" Tell Us

The "should be" and "rather be" questions work like a warning system. When there are too many yes answers to these questions, they tell us that something is out of balance.

With the "rather be's," too many yeses suggest that you are

dissatisfied with the activities that you have available to you. You would probably like to have other activities more available.

Too many "should be" yeses suggest some feelings of guilt or of doing something wrong when you are watching television.

The big question is "How many is too many?" The answer is "It depends." It depends on how much television you watch (the more you watch, the more yeses you can get); it depends on how you feel about television; in short, a lot of considerations. Try another approach. Look at the balance between yeses and noes as shown on Form D. Looking at the rather be question first, the easiest way to do this is to divide the total number of yeses from the rather be question into the total number of noes for the rather be question. Now, repeat the procedure for the should be question. Divide the total number of yeses for the should be question into the total number of noes for the should be question. If the answer is *2 or less* for either or both of the questions, maybe you have too many yeses. How about an example: If on the "rather be" question, I had six yeses and twelve noes, then six into twelve is two, which may signal too many yeses.

Well, okay, so what? Maybe I do have too many yeses. What does that mean? It may mean nothing at all. However, it might mean that I am not using television in the best way for me. Whichever the case, it suggests that talking this finding over with someone who listens well, and usually has good ideas, might be a good thing for me to do.

Part IV — The Apple-A-Day Instrument

The story about ourselves is just about complete. The Apple-A-Day instrument is the last part. To write this part of the story, we will use the "highest and lowest" technique on Form E. For each program you rated, find the dimension that scores the greatest amount of agreement from Form E. That would be the dimension with score *closest to 1.00.* Then, for that program, write into your narrative something like: "When I watched program _____ this time" (the "this time" reminds you that each time you do anything, it is, at least a little different from any other time) "the _____ dimension best described my reasons for watching" (use your name for the dimension.) "I _____ with the statements in that dimension." In this blank goes the words "agreed strongly" or "agreed" or "agreed slightly."

Which one of these three you use depends on the dimension score. If it is 1.00 or 1.33, use "agreed strongly." If it is 1.66 or 2.00, use "agreed." If it is 2.33 or 2.66, use "agreed slightly." If the dimension scoring closest to 1.00 has a value greater than 2.66, then the instrument did not have a good reason for watching in this case. Just drop this program out of this part of the narrative.

We are ready for the dimension disagreed with most. For each program, find the dimension whose score is closest to 5.00. Then write something like "When I watched program ＿＿＿＿ this time the ＿＿＿＿ dimension was the least descriptive of the reasons why I watched. I ＿＿＿＿ with the statements in this dimension." The last blank is filled in with "disagreed strongly" (5.00 or 4.67), "disagreed" (4.33 or 4.00), or "disagreed slightly" (3.66 or 3.33).

The last two statements we will write into the narrative come from the most-agreed-to and most-disagreed-with lists we just wrote. Take a look at the statements you wrote about the programs you viewed. Is there one dimension that appears most often in the most-agreed-with list? If there is, then you can write something like: "The most likely reason for watching television was described by the ＿＿＿＿ dimension." Look at your list of dimensions you disagreed with. If there is one dimension that appears more often than the others, write: "The least likely reason for watching television was described by the ＿＿＿＿ dimension."

THE PAYOFF

Your story is now complete. You now can speak, with *scientific evidence* to back you up, about the times that you watch, the programs that you watch, the programs that you like or dislike, whether changes in your emotional state or in your energy level occur while you are watching television, and about some of the reasons that describe why you watch and some of the reasons that are not descriptive. There are very few people, in fact, there are very few scientists, who can say that much.

Chapter 10

TELEVISION CITIZENSHIP: YOUR RIGHTS AND RESPONSIBILITIES

ALTHOUGH the major part of critical viewing skills education is concerned with the effective application of language skills, there is an important aspect of citizenship education that must be included. This concerns the public ownership of the "air," and the responsibilities of individual citizens to assure that both radio and television are used to promote the general welfare of our nation.

The section that follows here was written as a perspective for the study of regulatory agencies of the federal government, and for the study of censorship or other efforts to control the programming that is presented. It would appear important for students to gain an early appreciation of citizenship rights and responsibilities for a number of social institutions, including the radio and television stations in their communities.

In the material presented here, several objectives are considered:

1. An understanding of the foundations of U.S. radio/television programming, its history, economics, regulation, and operation.

2. The acquisition and comprehension of information regarding the development of radio/television as part of the natural resources that belong to all of the people.

3. The understanding of the relationship between FCC licensing of a local station and the expression of the citizens regarding the way the station serves the community.

4. The understanding of the process for expressing one's views of television to the local station and to the FCC.

Social studies objectives relating to history and government may be developed by the use of the material, and, of course, the actual writing of letters of commendation or criticism to local stations constitutes a practical language arts activity.

Radio and Television Programming: The Forces Behind the Set

Radio and television have become the most readily accessible forms of communication in the United States. In any home, in any U.S. city, at practically any hour of the day or night, and with little effort, it is possible to listen to the radio or to view television. Radio and television are an immutable part of our culture. They are daily praised and cursed. Their social impact and influences are debated by politicians, clergy, scientists, parents, and teachers. There is no question that broadcasting has changed America in its five decades; there is considerable argument as to what those changes are, whether they are good or bad, temporary or permanent.

This section explores programming, primarily television entertainment programming — the circumstances under which it is developed; the conditions under which it is viewed; and how we, the consumer, can effect changes in what we see.

The entertainment program that we see today on American television is a highly refined communication product that has been shaped by historical precedent, economic factors, and government regulation. Its historical precedents were in cinema and radio. The motion picture industry developed the methods of production, the cinemographic techniques of camera, sound, and editing. Radio developed the program format, the themes of entertainment, and the economic foundation of broadcasting. The economic realities of revenue and the income within a free enterprise philosophy have developed the structure of the industry by which programs are produced and distribution rights controlled. Government regulation brought service out of chaos in the early years of radio. Today the foundation of government influence is being rewritten in Congress. The potential impact of the result of that effort is as great as any we have seen. In order to establish the context of the entertainment program we will consider each of these areas briefly.

Historical Precedents — Film and Radio

From experiments in the late 1800s, motion pictures had become an industry by the first decade of the 1900s. Cinema cowboys in store front theaters were already choosing between their horse or girl in films shot on location in the wilds of New Jersey. The major cinematographic developments in pictorial composition and editing were well under way. Sound arrived in 1927. By the middle of the dreary thirties, movies were entertaining Americans with Wednesday dish nights and weekend nights on the town. When television began its rapid development following the end of World War II, the motion picture industry at first resisted and then capitulated, overrunning television with its content and technique. By the late 1950s the movies of the preceeding two decades were a staple throughout the broadcast day; live broadcasts of entertainment had virtually disappeared; most prime time programs were being done on film by the very studios that brought us Andy Hardy, Shirley Temple, and the rest.

Radio began its history as a means of communication for ships at sea and for wireless telegraphy. Public interest in the novelty was strong. When the patent agreements were reached in 1922, broadcast stations were built specifically to provide entertainment programs in order to stimulate the sale of radio receivers. It was AT&T, which held no rights to manufacture radio receivers, that invented the notion of the commercial sale of time. By the end of the 1920s the sale of time for commercial advertising was the primary source of revenue. Music was the lion's share of early radio, as it is now. The vaudeville variety show came next and then in the two decades prior to television, radio developed every program form that we now see. The literary concepts of continuing characters, serialization of plot, program length, and dramatic and comedic themes that are the foundation of television entertainment were adapted and developed during this period. Equally important, radio developed a pool of talent — writers, actors, producers on the creative side; salesmen, technicians, business executives on the management side — that would immediately grasp the implications of the invention of television. Finally, radio gave us networks. Technology and governmental regulation combined to limit the coverage area of the individual station to a radius of approximately 150 miles. The public demand for air time and rising program costs made it profitable for stations to sell blocks of time to program suppliers. These programmers could then sell commercial time to national advertisers who were less interested in the audience of any single station but were greatly interested in the extended coverage of the "network" of stations. The power of network programmers grew to dominate radio entertainment until the switch to television. That domination continues in television and is almost unchallenged during prime time hours.

Economic Factors

Commercial television in the United States is a revenue producing service. The Federal Communications Commission (FCC), which licenses stations, has decreed that this service shall be in the public's "interest, convenience and/or necessity." Stations on the other hand earn money by selling time to advertisers and to national networks. Commercial advertisers pay stations according to the size of the audience they deliver for their announcements. Networks pay stations according to the size of the market and the potential audience that market can deliver. Stations earn no money from the general public they are required to serve. This anomaly in the service to be provided and the source of income gives American commercial broadcasting its unique flavor. Commercial stations derive income directly from circulation — the number of individuals viewing. From an economic standpoint they are responsible to the advertisers, not the public. Like livestock traders, their job is to round up the herd by such means as are necessary and present it to the buyers for sale. The buyers, on their side, will inspect the herd to be sure it is of the kind and quality they want. The analogy may be crude, but it is not strained. We have had numerous instances in the industry where stations and networks have removed programming strictly on the basis of circulation. CBS, for example, removed a number of programs (Red Skelton was one) despite the fact that they drew a substantial audience. They were dropped because the audience they drew was of the wrong kind. It was older, beyond the 18 to 49 age bracket preferred by the advertiser.

To highlight the effect of a circulation-based revenue system on programming, consider the changes in program content that might occur if revenue was derived directly from the audience in the form of a use fee. Assume a program producer can produce a series of 10 programs for two million dollars. She wants to make a reasonable return on her dollar and looks to make three million total. In the present system she has to make the program appeal to a large, preferred audience of at least 20 to 25 million in order to make the four commercial time slots available in the program as attractive as possible to the advertiser. She must, in fact, get $75,000 a minute. In a use fee system it would only be necessary to find, say, 300,000 people to pay a dollar per program. In this latter system, specialized content becomes possible and likely. In the circulation-based system it cannot survive. Program producers, then, could begin to cater to smaller, more affluent audiences. Whether the less affluent would be served would depend on whether they exist in sufficient number to make low use fees profitable.

The fact that circulation is the economic core of commercial broadcasting affects not only the total program mix (it is the reason why at least 80 percent of all programming is entertainment) but also, each program within the mix — news is now happy talk because it generates higher ratings. Time and again we will turn to this economic base as an understanding for the style and structure of what we see.

Government Regulation

Once radio was returned to civilian hands following the end of World War I, it quickly grew into chaos. Stations changed frequency, power, and times of operation at will. Interference was the norm. Congress passed the Radio Act of 1927 establishing the Federal Radio Commission to bring order. The Federal Radio Commission became the Federal Communications Commission with the passage of the Communications Act of 1934. The FCC has the power to licence broadcast stations for a period of three years and to ensure that these stations serve the public "interest, convenience and/or necessity." Congressional action established that the public owned the broadcast spectrum and that stations were stewards of this trust. The FCC cannot censor, but it can impose fines or even lift licenses "after the fact" once a program has been broadcast. The FCC has no power over networks except through its licensing authority of the stations that belong to the network.

It is the licensing authority that has led social activist groups to petition the FCC to take action against a number of perceived program faults — violence, sex, advertising, biased news, and so forth. The FCC has thus far refused to take action on program content, fearing the role of governmental arbiter of public taste. The threat of this action, however, has caused broadcasters to band together in an industry organization called the National Association of Broadcasters (NAB). The NAB through its code of good practice has formulated rules of self-regulation, which have been remarkably responsive to public demands. The FCC's effect on program content has been described as "regulation by raised eye-brow." Stations are always aware that programming that offends a significant portion of the voting public may lead to a more active FCC.

There are other governmental agencies that impact on broadcasting. The National Telecommunication Information Agency (NTIA) is a policy formation group attached to the executive branch. The Federal Trade Commission (FTC) is charged with the responsibility of ensuring "Truth in Advertising" and has become active in proposing regulation of advertising directed toward children. The FTC has at various times proposed removing advertising directed at children under eight, removing all advertising for heavily sugared products, and restricting advertising during children's program times. These proposals have run into strong congressional opposition.

Structure of the Industry

Economic factors and government regulation have combined to form the present structure of the industry. The broadcast station provides the link between the public and the entertainment program, but it actually has little to do with the development or distribution of those programs. Governmental pressure has been brought to bear to separate the processes of development and distribution. While at one time networks did it all, now, there are a number of independent program producers who contract with networks to supply the series we see. A contract usually runs for a period of thirteen weeks. If the series generates sufficent circulation, the contract will be renewed for another thirteen weeks. At the end of these twenty-six weeks, the program goes into rerun. Network production of programs is currently limited to news, documentary, news magazine, and a very few entertainment programs (e.g. "The Tonight Show"). The networks, then, are primarily a distribution service. They buy time from stations in order to present the programs they have bought from the production houses. They sell time to national advertisers who present commercials during these programs. While the networks produce few of the programs, they certainly attempt to control the content of all they present. Independent producers of particularly successful programs may be able to force demands for "more artistic freedom," as long as circulation figures remain high, but the limits are clearly drawn.

In 1970 the FCC passed the Prime Time Access Rule, which limited network program viewing during prime time (7:00 P.M. to 11:00 P.M. EST) to three hours per night. This limitation permitted the further development of another system for distributing programs: syndication. A syndicated program is one that is sold on a market-by-market basis to individual stations for their exclusive use. Many daytime programs and almost all programs during the first hour of prime time are syndicated programs. Syndication has also offered a tentative challenge to network domination of other prime time hours in a few markets where program preferences run counter to the national norm.

The final source of programming in television is, of course, the local station. It has been the history of television that local programming has been in steady decline. It is now limited to local news, local inserts in movies (*Dialing for Dollars*) or syndicated programs, and an occasional talk show.

All programs live and die on the basis of ratings. Ratings are estimates of the number of people within a market or the nation who watch each and every program. There are two rating services in television, the A.C. Nielsen Co. and Arbitron. Both companies provide market-by-market estimates based on diaries, which are placed in volunteer homes initially selected from telephone directories. Respondents record the viewing of each member of the household for a period of one week. As far as the diaries are concerned, anyone viewing at least six minutes of a half-hour program has viewed it all. Both companies also have an overnight service in certain large cities (New York, Los Angeles, Chicago) where volunteer households have their sets connected by telephone to a computer, which records the time the set is on and the channel to which it is tuned. When the set is on the household is considered to be viewing the program tuned whether anyone is in the room or not. Finally Nielsen provides national ratings from a panel of about 1,200 respondents geographically selected to represent the U.S. pupulation. While new samples are drawn each time a ratings book is produced for the market-by-market survey, the national panel remains approximately the same from year to year with about 25 percent turnover.

Sampling procedures can be very accurate if the methods used do not systematically bias the selection of respondents. Unfortunately the methods used by the ratings companies are distinctly biased and systematically exclude representation for about 60 percent of the general population. Consequently statements about television being the most democratic of media or giving the people what they want have no basis in fact. As Dick Cavett is quoted as saying, "The people get what they get." The ratings are useful for making comparative statements (this program has more viewers than that one) — as long as it is understood that one is talking about a particular class of viewer.

Regardless of their limitations, ratings are an undeniable fact of television programming. No amount of pressure from special interest groups has been able to maintain a network program once its ratings have fallen (e.g. *Star Trek*) nor remove a successful one (e.g. *Soap*).

Pictures to come: Broadcast versus Broadband

For the past decade those of us who study television have read the revolutionary promises of broadband communication. Broadband communication is the term used for a communication service with virtually unlimited capacity to transmit electronic signals. These signals can become the newspapers, magazines, libraries, movie theatres, and personal telecommunicators of the future (for more discussion of the future, see Chapter 11). For the present, broadband communication is found in those homes that subscribe to a cable television service. That service typically provides excellent reception of local television stations and stations "imported" from other, distant markets. In recent months many of these cable companies have also subscribed to a movie service (e.g. Home Box Office). People who have "cable" pay a fee for the basic service plus additional charges for extra services such as movies.

In less than a dozen markets in the United States, cable companies are experimenting with a two-way service. The two-way transmission of information greatly increases the services that can be offered. Games can now be played with each player responding on a push-button device. Television-bingo has become popular. Tests and polls can be given. The questions are flashed on the screen and the individual responds by pushing a button corresponding to his answer. Two-way communication also permits the home receiver to order things. Shopping with catalogues can readily be accomplished. One could also order available movies or television programs to be relayed to the home set.

While such are possible, broadband communication has never met its promise. Its major effect has been to provide about 10 percent of the television homes with a few extra channels to watch or some more recent movies without commercials. Even this small service, however, has been shown to be profitable and to have had some impact on the programming of broadcast television. Representatives of broadcast television have expressed grave concerns that broadband television with its subscription fee economics might be able to outbid them for the best entertainment programming and sports. Up to now, the FCC has taken a protectionist stance, limiting the competition between broadband and broadcast television to the detriment of cable development.

What will the future bring? There seems little question that this is the last decade for television as we presently know it. The almost absolute control of television programming now exercised by network television will surely be broken by the team of cable and the home television recorder. A television producer who fails to sell her product to the networks will have two other outlets — the cable companies and sales direct to the home for playback on the home recorder. The additional sale outlets will mean that program content will become more diverse as appeals can be made to the tastes of specialized audiences. Programs sold to cable companies and directly to the home will be freed of the constraints of the FCC and of the networks standards and practices. Television programming consequently will become more controversial, daring, the extremes of good and bad pushed further out. As a result the individual will have more choices and will have to be more responsible in that decision making.

Radio and Television — The Rights of the Consumer

Because broadcasting makes use of a finite resource, the electromagnetic spectrum, it has come under governmental control. The "air waves" belong to the people who grant, through the licensing power of FCC, the use of that resource to corporations to provide service in the "public interest, convenience and/or necessity." The FCC assigns frequencies (potential stations) to each market, a geographical area usually identified by the major city within it. Licenses are granted to operate a broadcast station on these frequencies in a competitive hearing in which all petitioners present a complex statement on the services they will provide and document their ability to provide them.

This statement is a public document, a copy of which must be made available to any member of the public who presents himself during normal working hours and requests it. The request is binding and needs no explanation. In preparing the program proposal, the petitioner is required by the FCC to determine the needs of his community by surveying a sample of the general public and by contacting the leaders of the various "communities" within his service area. This formal process is known as "ascertainment," which is short for "ascertainment of community needs." The programming proposal, then, must reflect information from the ascertainment study and show how the programs and services that the petitioner is going to offer will meet the needs of the community.

In a public hearing the commission selects the proposal that in their judgment will best serve the public and grants a license for a term of three years. At the end of those three years the stations must petition for renewal. In that renewal petition the station must prepare a new programming proposal and again survey the community and its leaders to ascertain needs and desires. The renewal petition must also show how the performance of the station has met the promise of initial proposal.

In all of these proceedings, any citizen may "petition to deny" the granting or renewing of a station license. The petition to deny can be based on any number of elements, the character of the principals in the organization, the financial well-being of the corporation, the failure to provide service to significant minorities, and the like. In practice petitions to deny are rarely successful as the removal of a license is considered an executioner's stroke. There have, however, been some remarkable successes, which have forced broadcasters to higher levels of service.

Beyond the petition to deny, a citizen always has the right to complain to the station. By law the station must file the complaint in its public file and show in its next renewal its response. Its response may simply be an explanation of current practice and the reasons for its continuation. Complaints about programming have certain built-in restrictions. First, broadcast content is protected under the First Amendment of the Constitution. The FCC is specifically prohibited from censoring program material before it is aired. It can invoke fines or revoke a license for the broadcast of indecent obscene material, for example, after it has been aired. The most notable case in recent times was the George Carlin case, where a single citizen's letter of protest for the broadcast of what was considered obscene language resulted in the FCC issuing an order prohibiting its broadcast. That order was subsequently overturned by the court of appeals. Broadcasters, in general, have been very reluctant to find the limits of what they can broadcast but have been very aggressive in rebutting public complaints about indecency.

The second inherent restriction on complaints about programming is economic in nature. The selection of programming by stations and networks alike is almost always made on the basis of circulation. When a show is dropped it is ordinarily due to the ratings that it received. Complaints about dropped shows, then, have more than one strike against them from the outset. Even if the merits of the dropped program are outstanding, the FCC must question what public service is being offered by a program insufficient numbers of people watch.

The final limitation is against complaints about quality. Critics have bemoaned the lack of quality almost from the beginning of television. A critic writing in the very early fifties called television a "sea of mediocrity." It is the nature of television content that it is disposable; it is not to be savored and preserved for its lasting qualities. The industry has not been able to produce, nor has the audience shown any inclination to demand, works of literary value. Television programming and the popular music of radio have their moment and serve their purpose. Complaints about their quality are much like complaints against a house wine. If one wants vintage in either his beverage or drama he must be prepared to pay much more.

Successful complaints have dealt with programming that held classes of people up to ridicule, dealt with the news stories that were false or staged, and dealt with commercials that were misleading. To file a complaint, the individual would first write a letter to the station. The address is in the white pages of the telephone book. In the letter the individual should state the facts behind the complaint and then state what the station ought to be doing and why. The station will reply (assuming a name and address is supplied) and will file the letter in its public file, which the station must show to anyone who requests it. If the reply is not satisfactory the next letter should go to the Federal Communications Commission, 1919 M Street NW, Washington, D.C. 20554. This letter starts a proceeding that if pursued could lead to hearings on the renewal of the station's license.

A particular concern to the FCC are complaints that have to do with the fair presentations of ideas. Within the basic freedoms of this nation are the freedom of speech and the freedom of ideas. Speaking of the responsibilities of television in these areas, the U.S. Supreme Court issued the opinion that "it is the right of the public to receive suitable access to social, political, esthetic, moral and other ideas and experience." It is, therefore, the responsibility of each television station to provide exposure for ideas and issues. Different ideas often give rise to discussion and arguments. To ensure that all the many sides of each are presented, the FCC enforces a set of rules called the "Fairness Doctrine." The Fairness Doctrine requires that any controversial issue presented by a station be presented in a balanced manner. It was this rule that required the presentation of the anti-smoking commercials during the time that cigarette commercials were still permitted to be aired.

When the FCC considers complaints on fairness, it considers the balance of the presentations during the entire period that the issue was current. The FCC does not require an equal amount of programming on every side. It does require that all sides have fair access to the public during the issue's life span.

Finally, the FCC acts quickly on complaints concerning the equal time provisions for candidates for political office. No station is required to sell time for political advertising during a campaign (but it may be required to provide access under the Fairness Doctrine). If it does sell time to one candidate, it must sell an equal amount of time to all candidates for that office at the lowest rate. The Fairness Doctrine and the equal time provision are often confused. Fairness refers to fair access of controversial issues; equal time applies only to bona fide political candidates for the same office.

Cable Programming — The Rights of the Consumer

Programming presented over cable is not subject to review as broadcast programming is. The FCC does not license cable companies in the same manner that it provides a license for a broadcast station. Cable companies are awarded a franchise, usually by the local government agency in the community that will be served. That franchise document establishes the rate structure and the minimum service that will be provided by the company. Once a franchise has been awarded, the FCC will issue a certificate of compliance if the cable company meets the technical requirements for operation. Complaints concerning the operation of a cable company begin with the terms of the franchise. Many of these franchises were written with few demands on the cable company in order to get better "off-air" reception of distant television stations. Modern franchises make use of the increased competition between cable companies to ensure more services for the subscribers.

Beyond the franchise document, the rights of the consumer primarily reside in the ability to cancel the service and in the implied warrants established in law and precedent governing the relationships between consumer and provisioner. The operation of cable appears to be moving toward the notion of a common carrier. This concept relieves the distributor from responsibilities for the nature of the goods delivered. When viewed as a common carrier the cable company has no responsibility for the programming it delivers. That responsibility lies with the program producers who rent the cable channel to distribute their product. Despite the industry affinity for the common carrier status, some cable companies and many state communication agencies and utility commissions resist this position, holding instead that the cable company is an integral part of the communication service that it provides. It is responsible for the programming choices that it makes and must answer to the consumer for them. These issues are yet unresolved, or rather they are resolved in many different ways according to the individual states, local communities, and cable organizations involved in any particular case. The current federal inclination is to remove federal regulation to allow the marketplace to establish the conditions of operation.

Television, Citizenship, and the Classroom

Most television stations work hard to give us good entertainment, honest news, and ideas fairly presented. We do hear criticism of too much violence, too much sexually oriented material, too many commercials, and too little intellectual stimulation. As citizens we have the right and the responsibility to ensure that broadcast stations provide the service we want. A good beginning of the exercise of these rights and responsibilities is to conduct a careful study of just what is offered by the local television and radio stations. On television, this study starts with a composite week schedule. A composite week schedule draws a random Monday, Tuesday, and each of the other days of the week from the total year. The Monday might be in February, the Tuesday in August and so on. Each program that was shown on the date selected is logged in a regular television schedule. The composite week gives a good picture of what the overall service looks like. The schedule will show what percent of the programs are network supplied, come from syndication, or are locally produced. By applying a simple category scheme (see chapter 9), one can discover the relative proportion of entertainment in different forms, news, commentary, talk shows, and sports. The composite week gives good information for the next step, the review of the program proposal.

As we have noted stations must prepare a public document specifying the program service they will provide. The documents are complex and lengthy, but with mutual care and courtesy broadcasters will almost always work with teachers in providing the relevant portions for class work (in television a request for form 303 will generally suffice). The composite week and the program proposal allows for a comparison between promise and performance. Broadcast station managers as a rule enjoy talking about their business. Should questions arise in the comparison between the composite week and the proposal, it would be an excellent time in which to invite the manager.

The Communication Act of 1934 as amended is the repository of all citizen's rights to the air waves. The act has shown itself to be surprisingly resilent in dealing with the major technological changes that have occurred in communication. Your senator or representative can help you obtain a copy.

Investigating cable television is somewhat more difficult given the very local nature of cable reglulation. Each cable service, however, operates on a franchise. That franchise is usually negotiated with the local community, as we have noted. Assuming that there is a local cable service, the place to begin the search would be city hall. Most states also place cable service under the utilities commission or a communications agency. The management of the local cable service should be able to help identify the proper agencies.

Once the copy of the franchise has been obtained, it is good practice to document the services that *are* being provided and the services that *could* be provided. Services being offered to cable companies for distribution are expanding rapidly (one of the latest is a twenty-four hour music service with continuous rock concerts). The cable operator attempts to select those services that will garner the highest subscription rate with the lowest cost per subscriber. In the past, movies and better reception of off-air television have been the major selling point for cable television.

Television and radio provide unique circumstances where the ingrained interest in the content can lead to an exciting study of government economics and social responsibility. Radio and television belong to us, the people of the United States. In the end, if the students we teach exercise a little care and keep a watchful eye, we will all be well served.

Chapter 11

A LOOK INTO THE FUTURE

AS has often happened in the history of communication, we are again in an era where we have the technological capacity to make major changes in the means we use to communicate with one another. If we were to use the whole of this capacity, we could effect major changes in every social institution, revamp our transportation system, and even change the physical · arrangement of our cities. What of this capacity will actually be used depends on the creative innovation applied to those technologies and the level of competition present solutions provide. For example, a major retail chain had for years conducted its spring buying convention by hosting the buyers from all 610 stores at one major exhibition hall. As the company grew it had gotten more and more difficult to ensure that each buyer from each store would have sufficient time to review all the product lines the store carried. Further, costs for transporting, housing, feeding, and entertaining all the buyers for the several day run of the convention had risen beyond prediction. As these costs rose and the difficulties increased, the yearly convention turned into an overly expensive and unwieldy event. The chain turned to television, and in its own production studios, now produces videotapes of all the product lines. These tapes are sent to each of the stores for the buyers to select items they will stock. Even with high quality production, the cost is about one-quarter that of the convention. Economy, of course, is usually not enough to motivate major changes in the way we do things. In this example, change was directed first by the failure of the current method and by the innovativeness of the technological solution of the video presentation.

In this chapter we will consider the potential of near term developments in a communication system that has television as its central medium of delivery. We will focus attention on the potential impact of communication technology upon the life and work of the family. Technology available to us now and in use in, at least, some markets permits the delivery of television programs direct to homes from geosynchronous satellites, bypassing the need for broadcast stations or wired cities; permits full, two-way interchange of digital information[1] between homes on cable; permits us to show our own library of commercial movies, educational productions, and home-produced programs and coupled with the telephone allows buying directly from the home or office through the use of video catalogues. In the 1930s television was a proven technological capacity waiting to be properly marketed. In the 1980s we have a communication system that may find its place in our lives. Just how we do not know, but we can imagine as we do in this scene from a family home at the close of this century[2]

We enter the living room of the Wilson family in the late 1990s. Over in one corner is a television set that looks much like the one that we use today. The screen is larger, of course, and the case is now aluminum because wood has become so scarce. Grouped around the set are some other machines not usually found in our living rooms today. There seems to be a typewriter or some sort of keyboard alongside the set. The machine next to it rings a bell and begins to print out what appears to be the evening newspaper. Yes, there are the headlines, "OIL PRICES UP AGAIN!"

One of the children comes into the room, turns on the set, turns the channel to a picture title that says "Christmas toy catalogue." She turns on the typewriter and types in "Christmas toy catalogue request model trains." The picture flashes and on comes a man demonstrating engines, cars, and accessories for a model train set. "National Flyer is proud to show you its all new, jet powered engine. Totally safe for indoor use. To order, use the model number NF 1001. . . ." The girl watches the presentation, noting the items she wants to buy. Finally the announcer says, "This concludes your Christmas toy catalogue presentation on model trains." The picture returns to the "Christmas toy catalogue" title. The girl goes back to the typewriter. She types "Christmas toy catalogue order credit card number 54-312-7752. Identification number 307-04-1200."

The machine types back "credit OK identification registered. Please place your order."

---

[1]Digital information is the term for signals used to connect computers, work video games, provide teletext display — any video or audio other than picture and voice.

[2] The following material has been adapted from *Television and You* by J. Anderson and M. E. Ploghoft: Athens, Ohio, Ohio University Cooperative for Social Studies, 1975.

As she begins to type in her order, her mother calls from the kitchen, "Hurry up with the teletype, dear. Your father wants to order the groceries."

Now the toy order is complete; the machine types back. "Thank you for your order. All items *are* in stock. Delivery is scheduled tomorrow at one o'clock. Happy Holidays!"

As father walks into the living room, brother calls out "Hey, Dad, may I use the teletype just for a minute? I have to go to the library to get some information on this paper I am doing for social studies."

"OK" says Dad, "but hurry it up, the grocery store stops making deliveries at five o'clock."

"Right." The boy types "Library. School project number 044-316-112. Identification number 307-04-1300."

The typewriter responds: "Your public library is now at your service. Your name is Todd Wilson. You go to Wilamette Junior High School. Your teacher is Mr. Cramer. Your project is about television in the 1980s. Do you wish the standard research package, or do you have a special request?"

Todd types "special."

The typewriter answers, "You have a special request. Your teacher recommends that no special request be given unless the student has received the standard package. Have you received the package?"

Todd: "Yes."

Typewriter: "You have received the standard package. Please state your special request, using the procedures outlined in library publication number LP 101."

Todd (reading from the handbook): "Special request number 1. Book. Authors: Anderson and Ploghoft. Title: *Television and You.* End special request."

Typewriter: "Your special request has been received and will be sent to your printer in three minutes. Your paper is due on 1/15/99. Today's date is 12/18/98. You are very wise starting so early. Good luck."

"Dad! I'm all done."

"Thanks, Son."

Dad turns to channel 83, which shows the title "You Are What You Eat." He types, "Grocery order for Central Groceries" and then deftly enters his identification and grocery list. He types "Request fresh vegetable review." The TV screen flickers, a woman appears and says "This is Joan Williams, State Vegetable Inspector for Central Stores. The vegetables today at Central Groceries are from moderate to good quality. Prices are competitive to low. Best buys are in lettuce, celery and tomatoes. Mushrooms and romaine are overpriced for the quality. We will now begin our alphabetical review of each vegetable available."

Dad listens and types in his orders as each vegetable is shown and reviewed. At the conclusion he types "End of order." The typewriter answers "Central Groceries thanks you for your order. It will be placed on the next delivery truck which is scheduled at 4:45. Estimated time of arrival at your door is 5:15."

"Dad," Todd asks, "are you going to watch the movie tonight with us?"

"No, it is scheduled at 7:30 and my boss called a conference with the European buyers at 8:00 tonight. I will wait until it comes out on disc and get it from the library. Might even buy it if we all like it enough. Speaking of movies did you return that awful thing you were watching last night?"

"Yeah, I sent it back this morning."

"Well that's good."

"Sure, but I don't see why a 13-year-old kid can't make his own decisions on what to watch."

"Hey, usually you do and you make good ones too, but *The Night of the Claw*? Anyway, let's not go over all that again. Did the repairman come in to fix the telecommunicator upstairs in the office? The camera wasn't working well."

"Yeah, he was in. He was showing me how it worked. We talked to some guy in Germany who was repairing one there. When are we going to have one downstairs so I can talk to my friends?"

"Oh, come on, those things cost $100 a day. We wouldn't have one at all if my job didn't pay for it. What changes those things have made. Twenty years ago when I had a job in New York City, I had to *live* in New York City. Now, I live out here in the Ohio countryside. Never see the city."

Todd's mother walks in and says to Dad, "John, Leigh's teacher is sending her evaluation report out tonight on restricted Channel 1. We're scheduled for 6:30, can we make it?"

"That seems OK."

"Are you sure that no one else can see those evaluation reports? I would hate to have Mrs. Norton listening in."

"Um, they tell us that it comes to our home and only our home. If Mrs. Norton can see it, we'll sure find out about it."

That's the truth. Come on. Dinner is ready. Children, dinner is ready."

Todd: "Ahh, Mom, I'm right in the middle of a TV hockey game with Johnny Miller."

Mom: "Now you just type in the 'to-be-continued sign off' and come back to it after dinner."

"Hey, Johnny just typed in a forfeit. I win."

We leave this happy little family for what is still an old-fashioned dinner. The innovations that were projected in the scenario depend on some subtle and substantial changes in the way we currently do things. In general, we prefer our communication to be in one another's presence. Long distance telephoning is still advertised as "the next best thing to being there." We also like to physically hold and examine what we buy. "Going out" for an evening can add a special value to entertainment. Obviously, however, there are costs in the getting from here to there, costs in time, money, and effort. These costs seem to be increasing, and we may soon be unwilling or unable to pay them. The scenario was based on an analysis of those costs. We consider each more thoroughly here:

In our story, Leigh shops by video catalogue because the cost in paper resources, printing, and distribution even now are several times that of electronic distribution. But with cable penetration so low — less than a quarter of the homes in America are wired — there is no benefit for catalogue stores to put their selections on tape. Cable hook-ups will have to grow dramatically in the next twenty years for widespread video shopping to occur. There are many who question whether present raw materials are adequate for yet another wiring of America. It is possible, of course that wireless technology or laser technology will obviate the need for all that cable.

Leigh conducted her credit buying via electronic banking. In the brief period as she typed in her credit number and the computer responded her entire credit history was available. Had her account been seriously past due the transaction would have failed. This change seems inevitable and certainly more efficient than the telephone checks many stores practice today.

Todd's trip to the library is a simple update of the home encyclopedia. Schools working with libraries can program several resource works to be at the student's fingertips. The video disc, now being promoted for home movies, has thousands of frames on a side. Each frame can store a page of regular print or many pages in microprint. Complete libraries can be stored on a few discs. Whether we will have video books will depend on the response of printing technology and the publishing industry as well as our own feelings about the printed page. The video competition will be great. Current typographical computers allow the direct transfer from the author's typewriter to completed text without the single revolution of a printing press or even a single sheet of paper. Video libraries do not require large buildings and can be completely accessed by computer. However, who can browse among the grooves?

The grocery purchase is essentially a distribution solution, in the same way that the supermarket combined the trips to the butcher, baker, and candlestick maker into one efficient stop. Whether this change occurs depends on the human components of decision making. Our scenario calls for a surrogate shopper, one who will squeeze the tomatoes (if not the Charmin™) for us. There is no question that the lack of personal selection will lower quality in the home of the superior shopper. We can predict, however, stores advertising, "We pick your tomatoes better than your grandma did."

Todd's video disc imbroglio is happening in our more affluent homes today. Whether on tape, disc, cable, or over-the-air, programming will always be at issue. It is certainly likely that the concern with moral aspects of entertainment programs will continue, as will protests against commercials that mislead young viewers or induce them to buy nutritionally risky products. However, it seems that the advent of Home Box Office, video cassette and video disc programs, and the use of satellites to relay broadcasts from individual stations, such as WTBS/Atlanta, will have profound effects upon the variety and management of the program content that is shown on the family television sets.

Presently, the networks and local stations receive major criticism for programs and commercials considered offensive or inappropriate for young viewers. Soon, the parent will have responsibility for more supervision of the child's use of the television set, the parent will have primary responsibility for selection and purchase of the video disc programs that are then brought into the home. The explosion of the disc cassette industry will place responsibility where many persons feel it should always be: on the shoulders of individual parents. In any case, it seems clear that there will be a continuing need for children to be equipped with critical viewing skills, regardless of program sources.

Mr. Wilson's use of a telecommunicator transmitting his voice, picture, computer aided memos, letters, and data is the most radical of the projected changes. We base this projection on the internationalization and conglomerate growth of business. When regular business must be conducted in several locations at once, one's physical presence is no longer possible. Widely distant offices are now securely interlinked for data transmission. International teleconferencing is being used with increasing frequency, although problems in consistency and security of service are still to be solved.

Using restricted access channels, Leigh's teacher can prepare a video presentation on each of the students in class. The report can review progress, present test scores, show representative work, and also provide a tour of the classroom and school. Each home can be reached in the same way that each telephone can be dialed. With computer dialing, the whole presentation can be done automatically, leaving the teacher time to hold individual conference of some length with students of greater concern. Note that we have not predicted the demise of the "little red school house," although the communication system can certainly do a superior job of delivering information. As long as humans need to learn to be people as well as to learn the collected information and skills of the culture, the school and its teachers will be with us.

Our final prediction is the two-way interconnection of homes for digital information, which permits Todd and Johnny to play their hockey game, and lets the Wilsons get their newspaper electronically delivered. This interconnection depends on widespread cable penetration and high speed printers, of course, but solves the problem of the five day letter and the newspaper in the bushes. If we, the consumer, can learn to do without a hard copy (the paper itself) and to trust the continuous recall ability of a computer connected to a display screen (TV monitor), the entire business of printing is changed. The easy chair becomes a video command post and coffee tables appear where piles of magazines once rose.

This chapter has provided a quick look into the future, not so much to demonstrate an accuracy of prediction but to help illuminate the movement of our present communication system. The changes we have projected are essentially changes in the distribution system of goods and services and are based on the assumption that personal travel will get more costly and difficult. The content of television is also evolving. Content is becoming more diversified, following the direction set by magazines some thirty years before. There, specialty sheets (low circulation magazines that feature particular content) replaced the large circulation general interest periodicals like *Look, Life,* and *The Saturday Evening Post.* In television, the competition of independent stations, movie services, twenty-four hour specialty channels on cable, and home playback devices have ever so slightly slackened the stranglehold of the three commercial networks on prime time viewing. As of this writing, the network hold on the prime evening hours had declined by 6 percent. It is still a commanding 85 percent of television usage during those hours, but the decline is the first in the history of television.

Clearly, we are moving into a time of more choices being available to the television audience. The next decade should see the regular provision of ten to fifteen channels in every market, to suggest a very conservative number. That number of channels, given a typical eighteen hour program day, will require almost 1,500 hours of program material per week. This demand will be filled by many different types of content from the instructive to the, at least, softcore pornographic.

The two forces of channel demand and program material demand are applying steady pressure to the present system of delivery of television services via broadcast stations. Broadcasting — the sending out of radio signals — is a technology some thirty years out of date. It is a very wasteful use of a valuable resource — radio spectrum space. There is a finite section of the electromagnetic spectrum that can efficiently be used for sending out signals of any kind, radio telemetry, satellite communication, and even citizen band conversations. One use of a given frequency generally precludes any other. Broadcast television uses an enormous chunk of that spectrum, which would be freed for other uses if the television service could be delivered through cable, fiber optics, or laser technology.

The change from broadcasting to some other form of delivery would have little impact on the audience except for the increase in channel capacity, but would have substantial impact on broadcast stations and networks. Commercial broadcasters as the controlling link between content and the audience are essentially time brokers, selling access to an audience in units of ten, thirty, and occasionally sixty second slots for commercial messages. If programming is distributed through some other technology, broadcast stations will have nothing to sell. Forecasting this potential turn and the steadily increasing demand for program material, the more aggressive stations are turning into production houses. They are returning to the actual production of television programs, an activity they all but left behind in the mid 1950s.

Networks, which, in fact, are nothing more than paper companies that use the buying power of their affiliate stations to purchase programming (the engineering aspects of distribution are pretty much handled by AT&T), have also begun to adapt. They will remain as supply companies commissioning and selling programming to one and all. CBS has, for example, recently formed a cultural programming service for cable companies.

Programming at the local level may also see a dramatic increase. The dream of locally produced television programming has never become a reality in spite of a number of regulatory attempts by the Federal Communications Commission (FCC). From its inception as the Federal Radio Commission, the FCC has espoused the notion of local service. It did so in the initial allocations of stations to markets, in its programming category requirements, in its now rescinded requirement for cable companies to provide local production facilities and channels and in its prime time access rule, which prohibits networks from supplying programming for all the prime time hours. The marketplace has continually stymied that regulatory goal. We, the audience, have shown little interest in locally produced programming. That programming simply could not compete with network or syndicated fare. The FCC is trying once again to promote local service by authorizing a class of low powered broadcast television stations. While there is yet no practice, in theory almost every community of any size could now have its very own television station. The technology for these stations is relatively inexpensive; 50 to 100 thousand dollars will put one on the air. What these stations will broadcast and how they will derive income is, of course, unknown. One speculation is that they will become the local, commercial, electronic newspaper. It is also quite possible that this attempt at localism will also fail.

Even if little of our technological capacity is adopted, changes in content will continue to occur. Historically, particular content in television has shown cycles of popularity and disinterest. The western has come and gone and may be coming back in the historical novel form. The present sexually primed situation comedy is beginning to ebb, being replaced by perhaps, the more "cerebral" shows like *Hill Street Blues* or the soapy "adult" themes of *Dallas* or most likely by a crazy quilt pattern of many types. Trends in programming can usually be traced in the rating reports given by the television correspondent or critic reporting in the local newspaper. Analysis of these trends is a very useful classroom activity.

In examining the future the interlocking nature of our own sociological and technological institutions comes clearly into view. Space technology in the computer chip and the transistor has made major changes in television production and distribution, at the same time placing strong demands for the spectrum space that television occupies. The cost of personal travel has motivated the development of better long distance communication links, which in turn require the basic petroleum and metallic resources for the cable and satellite connections. Change in one area, then, predicts change in many areas. What will remain of our present system? Our individual requisite for contact with one another in face-to-face communication will remain. However powerful or complex our media become, as long as we are to be human, the communication between parent and child, brother and sister, teacher and student, person to person, will be paramount.

READINGS AND RESOURCES

A categorical bibliography providing an introduction to television.

General Works

Advertising: The image maker. Columbus, OH: Xerox Education Publication, 1974.

Anderson, C. *The electric journalist: An introduction to video.* New York: Praeger Publishers, 1974.

Anderson, J. A. and Meyer, T. P. *Man and communication.* Washington, D.C.: College and University Press, 1974.

Bowers, R. T. *Television and the public.* New York: Holt, Rinehart and Winston Inc., 1973.

Budd, R. W. and Ruben, B. D. *Beyond media: New approaches to mass communication.* Rochelle Park, NJ: Hayden, 1979.

Dondis, D. A. *A primer of visual literacy.* Cambridge, MA: MIT Press, 1979.

Head, S. W. *Broadcasting in America.* 2nd Edition. Boston: Houghton Mifflin, 1972.

Heintz, A. C., Reuter, L. M. and Conley, E. *Mass media: A worktext in the processes of modern communication.* Chicago: Loyola University Press, 1975.

Kuhns, W. *Exploring television.* Chicago: Loyola University Press, 1975.

Pember, D. R. *Mass media in America.* Chicago: Science Research Associates, Inc., 1974.

Ploghoft, M. E. and Anderson, J. A. *Education for the television age.* Springfield, Ill.: Charles C Thomas, 1981.

Aesthetics, Forms and Formulas

Cheseboro, J. W. and Hamsher, C. D. Communication values and popular television series. *Journal of Popular Culture,* 1974, *8,* 589/3-603/17.

Cohn, W. H. History for the masses: Television portrays the past. *Journal of Popular Culture,* 1976, *10,* 280-289.

Gans, H. J. *Popular culture and high culture: An analyses and evaluation of taste.* New York: Bantom, 1974.

Glut, D. F. and Harmon, J. *The great television heroes.* Garden City, NJ: Doubleday, 1975.

Madden, D. The necessity for an aesthetics of popular culture. *Journal of Popular Culture,* 1973, *7,* 1-13.

Nachlar, J., Weiser, D. and Wright, J. L. (Eds.). *The popular culture reader.* 2nd ed., Bowling Green, Ohio: Bowling Green Popular Press, 1978.

Newcomb, H. *Television: The critical view;* New York: Oxford University Press, 1976.

Newcomb, H. *TV: The most popular art.* Garden City, NY: Anchor Books, 1974.

Zettl, H. Toward a multi-screen television aesthetic: Some structural consideration. *Journal of Broadcasting,* 1977, *21,* 5-20.

Zettl, H. *Sight, sound, motion: Applied media aesthetics.* Belmont, CA: Wadsworth, 1973.

Images

Aronoff, C. Old age in prime time. *Journal of Communication,* 1974, *24,* 86-87.

Asante, M. K. Television and black consciousness. *Journal of Communication,* 1976, *26,* 137-141.

Cantor, J. R. Television's portrayal of minorities and women. *Journal of Broadcasting,* 1977, *21,* 435-446.

Jeffres, L. W. and Hur, K. K. White ethnics and their media images. *Journal of Communication.* 1979, *29,* 116-122.

Roberts, C. The portrayal of black on network television. *Journal of Broadcasting,* 1970-71, *15,* 45-53.

Integration Into Curricular Areas

Kean, John M. and Personke, Carl. Chapter 12: "Media." *The Language Arts.* New York: St. Martin's Press, Inc., 1976.

Ploghoft, Milton E. and Shuster, A. H. *Social Science Education in the Elementary School.* Columbus: Charles E. Merrill, 2nd ed., 1976, chapter 12.

Rice, S. and Mukerji, R., Eds. *Children are centers of understanding media.* Washington, D.C.: Association for Childhood Education International, 1973.

Schronk, J. *TV action book.* Evanston, Ill.: McDougal Littell and Co., 1974.

Wylie, Eugene D. and Warmke, Roman F. *Free enterprise in the United States.* Cincinnati: South-Western Publishing Co., 1980.

WNET/thirteen, *Critical Television Viewing: A Language Skills Work-a-Text.* New York: Cambridge, 1980.

Media and the Classroom

Hilliard, R. L. and Field, H. Television and the teacher: *A handbook for classroom use.* New York: Hastings House, 1976.

Kaye, E. *The ACT guide to children's television, or how to treat tv with TLC.* Boston: Beacon, 1979.

Littell, J. F. *Coping with the mass media.* Evanston, Ill.: McDougal Littell and Co., 1972.

Littell, J. F. *Coping with television.* Evanston, Ill.: McDougal Littell and Co., 1973.

Media now. Red Oak, Iowa: Southwest Iowa Learning Resources Center, 1975.

Rice, S. and Mukerji, R., Eds. *Children are centers for understanding media.* Washington: Association for Childhood Education International 1973.

Schronk, J. *TV action book*. Evanston, Ill.: McDougal Littell and Co., 1974
Valdez, J. and Grow, J. *The media works and working with the media works*. Dayton, OH: Plfaum/Standard, 1973.
White, N. *Inside television: A guide to critical viewing*. Palo, Alto, CA: Science and Behavior Books, Inc., 1980.

Media Effects

Baran, S. J., Chase, L. J. and Courtright, J. A. Television drama as a facilitator of prosocial behavior: "The Waltons." *Journal of Broadcasting*, 1979, *23*, 277-284.
Cohen, A. A. and Salomon, G. Children's literate television viewing: Surprises and possible explanations. *Journal of Communication*, 1979, *29*, 156-163.
Comstock, G., Chaffee, S., Katzman, N., McCombs, M. and Roberts, D. *Television and human behavior*. New York: Columbia University Press, 1978.
Cox, H. The consciousness industry: A theological view of the media. *Public Telecommunications Review*, 1973, 1, 8-15.
Sprafkin, J. N. and Rubenstein, E. A. Children's television viewing habits and pro-social behavior: A field correlational study. *Journal of Broadcasting*, 1979, *23*, 265-276.

Production Techniques

Burstein, H. *Questions and answers about tape recordings*. Blue Ridge Summit, Penn.: TAB Books, 1974.
Millerson, G. *Techniques of television production*. New York: Hastings House, 1968.
Millerson, G. *The technique of lighting for television and motion pictures*. New York: Hastings House, 1972.
Millerson, G. *TV camera operation*. New York: Hastings House, 1973.
Mitchell, W. *Televising your message: An introduction to television as communication*. Skokie, Ill.: National Textbook Co., 1974.
Westmoreland, R. *Teleproduction shortcuts: A manual for low budget television products*. Norman, Okla.: University of Oklahoma Press, 1974.

Program Types

Adams, W. C. and Ferler, P. H. Television interview shows. *Journal of Broadcasting*, 1977, *21*, 141-151
Adler, R. P. (Ed.) *All in the family: A critical appraisal*. New York: Praeger, 1979.
Gans, H. J. *Deciding what's news: A study of CBS Evening News, NBC Nightly News, Newsweek and Time*. New York: Pantheon Book, 1979.
Novak, M. The game's the thing: A defense of sports as ritual. *Columbia Journalsim Review*, 1976, *15*, 33-38.
Prisuta, R. H. Televised sports and political values. *Journal of Communication*, 1979, *29*, 94-102.
Smith, R. R. Mythic elements in television news. *Journal of Communication*, 1979, *29*, 75-82.

Stedman, R. W. *The serials: Suspense and drama by installment.* Norman: University of Oklahoma Press, 1977.

Tuckman, G. *Making news: A study of the construction of reality.* New York: Free Press, 1978.

Williams, C. T. It's not so much you've come a long way baby — as you're gonna make it after all. *Journal of Popular Culture,* 1974, *7*, 984-990.

INDEX

189